CLEAN START

CLEAN START

100 RECIPES TO INSPIRE YOU TO EAT CLEAN AND LIVE WELL

TERRY WALTERS

Photography by Gentl & Hyers

STERLING EPICURE
New York

STERLING EPICURE
New York

An Imprint of Sterling Publishing
387 Park Avenue South
New York, NY 10016

STERLING EPICURE is a trademark of Sterling Publishing Co., Inc.
The distinctive Sterling logo is a registered trademark of Sterling Publishing Co., Inc.

This edition published in 2014.

ISBN 978-1-4549-1350-4

Distributed in Canada by Sterling Publishing
C/o Canadian Manda Group, 165 Dufferin Street
Toronto, Ontario, Canada M6K 3H6
Distributed in the United Kingdom by GMC Distribution Services
Castle Place, 166 High Street, Lewes, East Sussex, England BN7 1XU
Distributed in Australia by Capricorn Link (Australia) Pty. Ltd.
P.O. Box 704, Windsor, NSW 2756, Australia

For information about custom editions, special sales, and premium and corporate purchases,
please contact Sterling Special Sales at 800-805-5489 or specialsales@sterlingpublishing.com.

Manufactured in Canada

10 9 8 7 6 5 4 3 2 1

www.sterlingpublishing.com

The information in this book is provided as a resource for inspiration and nutritional education.
It is not prescriptive, but may be used to complement the care of a qualified health professional.
Author and Publisher expressly disclaim responsibility for any adverse effects from the use or
application of the information contained in this book. Neither the Publisher nor Author shall
be liable for any losses suffered by any reader of this book.

Designed by MacKenzie Brown Design
Chicago, Illinois
www.mackenziebrown.com

Photography by Gentl & Hyers
New York, New York

Dedicated with love
to Mom and Dad,
for making it possible
from the start.

SHARING THE JOURNEY

To all who have attended my programs and classes over the years, have connected through my blog or Facebook, have purchased CLEAN FOOD, or are discovering me and my passion just now as you turn these pages...thank you for being part of my journey.

Special thanks to Andrea Gentl and Marty Hyers for their talent and vision, and for showing clean food in all its natural beauty. Andrea, Marty, Meredith, Heidi, Helen, Alpha, Molly, Emma, Rob and Kacy – it was an honor to work with you and I thank you from the bottom of my heart.

I am blessed to have dear friends – all of whom cannot be thanked enough for enriching my life with their love and support. Special thanks to Pam Powell, Maria and Peter Uzzi, Sue Davies, Beth Zapatka, Susan Case, Nancy Frodermann and the running buddies with whom I've shared so many miles.

To my amazing and caring family: Gary Jacobs, David and Fernanda Jacobs, Barbara Gadd and my nieces and nephews. And to my mother and father who fuel me with their incredible energy, purpose, support and love. Living this dream is made all the more special by sharing it with you.

To Mike Kandefer and Urban Oaks Organic Farm, for growing incredible organic produce, and for creating a sustainable, delicious and clean future.

To Tony Gardner, my dear friend, agent, and publishing tour guide for making it "all part of the service!"

To Mightybytes, the greatest web team ever, and to Carol Leggett Public Relations for being so responsive, supportive and forward thinking.

To Marcus, Carlo, Jason, Leigh Ann, Jeff, Meaghan and the entire Sterling Publishing team for taking clean to heart, and giving me a platform from which to share it with so many others.

To Tracey Ryder and Edible Communities for so warmly welcoming me into your publishing family.

To Kurt MacKenzie, Andrew Brown and the entire MacKenzie Brown Design team. Thank you for being the greatest designers and friends. I couldn't imagine sharing this ride with anyone else.

To Andrew Brown. There's no way I could possibly thank you enough for your partnership, your friendship, your support and your love.

To Stöckli, my most loyal friend and running partner, because Sarah and Sydney insisted that you have a place in this book. Good boy!

To Chip, Sarah and Sydney, who have not only shared this incredible adventure, but who have made it possible and worthwhile. Thank you for supporting me and my dreams. You nourish my heart and soul, and I am so blessed to have you.

CONTENTS

CLEAN START

is about enjoying healthy, delicious, clean food every day. It's about having a relationship with food that's not based on living up to somebody else's ideal, or following a strict regimen. It's simply about making healthy choices, one at a time, and doing the best that you can do, empowered with knowledge and motivated by intention. It's about maximizing nutritional value and taste, and minimizing waste and imbalance. It's about true nourishment. The kind that makes you feel good about yourself. The kind you want to share with others. CLEAN START is about YOU living a delicious, vibrant and sustainable life. There's no better place to start than exactly where you are. This is your guide. This is your clean start.

Clean food is whole, minimally processed and close to the source for maximum nutrition. This is the food we all need more of, no matter what else is on your plate. This is the food that allows you to live a healthy life, and to accomplish what you want without the limitations that result from compromised nutrition and health. Whether you're starting again or starting anew, eating clean is about being nourished by your food and by your journey.

EAT CLEAN. LIVE WELL.

Terry

START HERE

It doesn't matter where you are starting. Eating clean is about what we can do now to make healthy choices that are simple, nutritious and delicious. This is the perfect time and place for your clean start.

You don't have to deprive yourself of your favorite foods, or feel bound by rigid or unreasonable guidelines. A clean start has to fit your unique constitution and lifestyle, not set you up to fail. All you have to do is enjoy good, clean food, one recipe at a time, and all the other pieces and health benefits that go along with it will follow. Who doesn't want that?! Whatever your motivation, here's to you and your clean start, and here's to sharing and enjoying the journey.

EAT THE COLORS OF THE RAINBOW.

The more colorful your diet, the more nutrient-rich. Go easy on empty white filler foods and heavy on healing greens.

EAT DARK LEAFY GREENS EVERY DAY.

For me, green is the most important color and the one most lacking in our diets. Greens are cleansing, healing, uplifting, and rich in calcium and minerals. Try using a variety of greens to amp up the nutritional value of your salads, soups, sauces, stir-fries and even smoothies. Just get them in!

EAT ALL FIVE TASTES.

Sweet, sour, salty, bitter and pungent are all found naturally and nutritionally in clean food, as opposed to manufactured "natural flavors" and the imbalance of sweet and salty tastes found in processed foods.

EAT FOODS THAT ARE GROWN, NOT MANUFACTURED.

Clean food comes from a green plant, not a processing plant – a farm, not a factory.

SKIP THE PACKAGE.

A package is the first sign that you've moved away from the source. Look for foods that don't require a label to reveal what's inside; but if it comes in a package, apply the "grown not manufactured" tip when reading labels.

BUY CLEAN FOOD AND LEAVE THE REST BEHIND.

Make the difficult choice just once at the store so you're not faced with making it every time you open your cupboard.

BUY AND TRY ONE NEW CLEAN FOOD EACH TIME YOU SHOP.

If you don't know where to begin, start with something green! One new clean food a week and by the end of a year you'll be feeling the benefits of eating clean and living well.

KNOW THE SOURCE OF YOUR FOOD.

Make friends with your grocer, your farmer and your local producers. Understanding where and how food was grown or produced is essential to making healthy choices.

BUY LOCAL AND ORGANIC WHEN YOU CAN.

Clean food is fresh and nutrient-rich. What you see is what you get – without a host of unwanted contaminants and byproducts that often accompany conventional growing, processing and shipping.

BE NOURISHED BY YOUR FOOD AND MAKE PEACE WITH YOUR CHOICES.

Make conscious choices, enjoy every bite and let your food and mealtime nourish your entire being.

A SUCCESSFUL CLEAN START

...IS DIFFERENT FOR EVERYONE.

For one person, eating clean may mean eliminating preservatives and artificial ingredients. For the next, it may mean giving up processed foods altogether. And for yet another, it may mean going directly to the farm. What matters most is not where you are in this continuum, but that you identify opportunities to move closer to the source and are empowered to act on them.

...IS RICH WITH THE FOODS WE ALL NEED MORE OF.

The recipes in this book are free of meat, dairy, gluten and refined sugar, and rich in whole grains, fresh produce, non-animal sources of protein, and healthy and essential fats. No matter what your dietary preference, everyone at your table will enjoy the tastes, the variety and the nourishment from your clean food creations.

...NOURISHES AND SATISFIES.

Clean food nourishes your senses and satisfies your nutritional needs. It looks, smells, tastes and is delicious. It deepens your connections – to the environment, to the source of your food, to your community and to your self, allowing you to serve your unique needs and support good health in a balanced and sustainable way.

...INSPIRES US TO EAT CLEAN AND LIVE WELL.

So many factors go into decisions about what to eat – from taste and ease, to health and beliefs. Success is not obtained by jumping from one extreme to another, but rather by making conscious choices based on all these factors. Share the journey, nourish yourself with all that life has to offer, and your clean start will feed your soul and inspire others.

BENEFITS OF A CLEAN START

THE BEST BENEFIT OF A CLEAN FOOD DIET IS THAT YOU'RE GOING TO LOVE YOUR FOOD AND YOUR MEALTIME. HERE IS JUST A SMALL SAMPLE OF WHAT ELSE YOU STAND TO GAIN.

POTENTIAL BENEFITS	IMPACT ON ENVIRONMENT
Increased energy and vitality	Less packaging
Strengthened immune system	Less waste
Reduced inflammation	Less contamination
Reduced acidity	Improved local environment and economy
Greater heart health	Increase in local jobs
Improved mental focus	
Reduced risk of diabetes	Maintains unique local foods
Healthy weight control	Maintains crop diversity
Better absorption of vitamins and minerals	Creates a sustainable food system
Less exposure to genetically modified foods, pesticides and growth hormones	Less overproduction of soy, corn and beets
Fewer complications from food sensitivities	Less dependence on genetically modified food

ONE HEALTHY CHOICE AT A TIME IS ALL IT TAKES TO SUPPORT GOOD HEALTH FOR YOURSELF AND THE ENVIRONMENT.

CLEAN START KITCHEN

Just as every body is unique, so is every kitchen and cook. To make your clean start as enjoyable, easy and successful as possible, here are some recommended ingredients and tools. The goal of a clean start is not to jump from one extreme to another, but rather to make a slow and successful change over time. Just one new clean food or CLEAN START recipe per week, and at the end of a year your clean start will have transitioned to long-lasting habits that fuel a healthy life.

TOOLS

QUALITY SHARP KNIVES AND GRATERS One quality 8-inch chef's knife and a standard box grater can accomplish many of the tasks in my recipes.

CAST IRON SKILLETS are naturally non-stick, heat and cook evenly, are a breeze to clean and turn out great results every time – especially when you're looking to caramelize. If you don't have or care for cast iron, stainless or enameled skillets will also work.

DUTCH OVENS are so multipurpose that I find I need little else. An enameled finish is non-stick and easy to clean, and a 4½ quart Dutch oven accommodates most of my soups and sautés. Similar sized pots with lids can be substituted.

GLASS CONTAINERS AND MASON JARS make great clean storage for whole grains, legumes, nuts, seeds, spices and more. It's not necessary to keep every item on hand, but a rotating selection from each category will give you great variety and options. Quantities in excess of what you might use in a few weeks should be stored in the freezer for maximum shelf life.

HANDHELD BLENDERS (also called immersion blenders) have nearly replaced the food processor in my kitchen. They're relatively inexpensive, can be used for a variety of tasks and are easy to use, clean and store. You can also use a food processor, blender or a whisk with some muscle behind it!

RICE COOKERS are my saving grace and ensure that I won't be reminded of my cooking grain when I smell it burning. Avoid rice cookers with exposed aluminum interiors. Stainless-steel rice cookers are my preference. If you have difficulty finding them in stores, look online. Pressure cookers or appropriate sized pots can easily be substituted.

CLEAN START PANTRY

WHOLE GRAINS

Amaranth

Barley*

Brown rice
(whole grain and flour)

Cornmeal

Millet

Oats*
(whole, steel cut, rolled)

Quinoa
(ivory and/or red)

Teff
*(ivory and brown –
whole grain and flour)*

Wild rice

VEGETABLES AND FRUITS

In addition to seasonal fresh produce, here are some other year-round staples:

Dried fruits
(apricots, cherries, cranberries, dates, raisins…)

Dried sea vegetables
(arame, kombu, nori)

Dried shiitake mushrooms

Garlic

Lemons/lemon juice

Limes/lime juice

Onions

Pickles

Sun-dried tomatoes
(dried, not packed in oil)

LEGUMES

Dried legumes can be prepared in advance and frozen for later use, while canned legumes are a great backup on days when you just don't have time.

Aduki beans
(also adzuki)

Black beans

Cannellini beans

Chickpeas

Fava beans

Great northern beans

Kidney beans

Lentils

Navy beans

Pinto beans

Red beans

Split peas

NUTS, SEEDS AND BUTTERS

Almonds
(nuts and butter)

Cashews
(nuts and butter)

Pecans

Pumpkin seeds

Sesame seeds
(ivory and black)

Sunflower seeds
(and butter)

Walnuts

OILS

Extra virgin olive oil

Grapeseed oil

Sesame oil
(toasted and/or hot)

Virgin coconut oil

VINEGARS

Apple cider vinegar

Balsamic vinegar

Brown rice vinegar

Red wine vinegar

Ume plum vinegar

SWEETENERS

Apples/applesauce

Bananas

Brown rice syrup

Maple syrup

Molasses

FLOURS

Almond meal

Arrowroot

Chickpea flour
(garbanzo bean flour)

Corn flour

Potato starch

Tapioca flour

Teff flour
(ivory and brown)

SPICES AND MISCELLANEOUS

Baking powder
(aluminum- and gluten-free)

Baking soda

Braggs Liquid Aminos

Chile powder

Cinnamon

Ginger root

Grapeseed oil mayonnaise

Mirin
(brown rice cooking wine)

Miso paste
(found in the refrigerated section)

Nutmeg

Pepper

Sea salt
(fine and course grinds)

Shredded coconut

Tamari
(natural wheat-free soy sauce)

*contains gluten

THE BASICS

When it comes to eating clean and living well, the most powerful tools we have are intention and the ability to make the choices that serve our best interests. Together, these tools can help us navigate our way through grocery stores, restaurants, and a variety of temptations. But when I'm cooking in my kitchen, my goal is much more basic – to bring together tastes, textures, colors and nutrients to create meals that all will enjoy. I think of my cast-iron skillet as my palette, clean food as my paint, and my finished dishes as the resulting creation that brings together and nourishes my family and friends.

Whether you follow my recipes to a T or vary them with your own creative spirit, these basic recipes and tips will help you get started eating minimally processed, nutrient-rich, clean food that supports good health and balance in a delicious way. And if you're interested in additional information about the health benefits of a variety of foods and cooking techniques, plus more recipes that satisfy, then you'll also enjoy my first cookbook, CLEAN FOOD.

FINDING CLEAN FOOD

Maximum nutrition, freshness and taste come from locally grown, in-season vegetables and fruits. Your fresh produce will vary from week to week and season to season. It could come from your grocer, your farmer, a farmers market, a share in a CSA (Community Supported Agriculture) or your very own garden. In fact, sometimes I think that the pursuit of clean food is every bit as enjoyable as eating it!

This is the perfect opportunity to discover your unique local foods, to connect with your community and the land and to support your local farmers and economy. If you're not sure where to find resources for clean food near you, a quick trip to your local library, department of agriculture or the Internet is a great place to start. While there are many websites and resources available, here are just a few of my favorites to help you get started.

SLOW FOOD www.slowfood.com
LOCAL HARVEST www.localharvest.org
ENVIRONMENTAL WORKING GROUP www.ewg.org
AMERICAN FARMLAND TRUST www.farmland.org

With local resources identified and a well-stocked pantry, you are well on your way to enjoying a cornucopia of fresh, seasonal produce with ease. Let the CLEAN START adventure begin!

INGREDIENTS

ALMOND MEAL/FLOUR is a great addition to baked goods, as it packs them with protein and nutrients and produces a moist result. Almond meal is available at most health food stores or can be prepared at home using a food processor or coffee grinder. Process or grind blanched or raw almonds until they resemble flour. Pour through a sifter or mesh strainer and tap into a separate container. Place any large pieces that did not go through back in the processor or grinder and process again. Repeat until you have an even, flourlike consistency.

ARROWROOT is a natural starch and thickening agent that comes in powder form. It's available in most natural food stores. Substitutes include tapioca flour, kudzu or cornstarch.

GINGER ROOT A porcelain grater allows you to capture and use the natural juices as well as the grated root. A microplane or stainless steel grater also works just fine. Much of the skin from the root will peel back on its own as you grate, so it's not necessary to peel it first unless you prefer no skin at all.

GOMASIO is a condiment made from grinding together sesame seeds and salt. You can make it yourself or purchase it prepared at most natural foods stores.

KOMBU is a sea vegetable that imparts significant health benefits when used. A small piece (about the size of your thumb) added to whole grains and legumes will reconstitute in the cooking water and infuse grains and legumes with minerals. Kombu also neutralizes the acid-forming property of grains, and tenderizes and reduces the gaseousness of legumes.

LEEKS look like extra-large scallions but have a slightly sweeter taste. To prepare, trim and discard root end, rinse leeks well and use the white and light green parts only. The dark green parts are bitter.

MISO is made from fermented soy and is a living food that helps replenish healthy intestinal flora. It's important not to allow miso to boil, as its health benefits are destroyed by high temperatures. When preparing leftovers, reheat soup separately, remove from heat, dissolve miso in warm water and stir into individual servings. Mellow white varieties of miso (such as brown rice and chickpea) have been fermented for one year and are milder than three-year fermented varieties.

RICE MILK is my milk substitute of choice. I like that it has less added sugar and oil than other milk alternatives, and my children like it the best. You can substitute hemp milk, almond milk, coconut milk, goat milk or cow milk to suit your preference.

TOFU, made from soybeans, is a rich source of protein that comes in two varieties. Silken tofu, also known as Japanese-style tofu, whips smooth and can be used to make dressings, puddings and creams. Regular tofu, or Chinese-style tofu or bean curd, holds its shape, can be roasted, grilled or added to a stir-fry (this is the variety I like to crumble into my lasagna). Both varieties come in soft, medium, firm and extra-firm. Regular tofu is found in the refrigerated section, whereas silken tofu is often sold in shelf-stable packaging.

VEGETABLE STOCK is an easy way to amp up the flavor and nutritional value of your recipes – from soups and stews to grains and legumes. Stock can be made in advance and stored in the freezer. You can also use the infused water from steaming vegetables or from soaking sea vegetables, dried tomatoes or dried mushrooms. There are many vegetable stocks available that eliminate the need to make your own. Look for brands that list only vegetables in the ingredient list, and that have minimal salt (if any), and no preservatives. When all else fails, substitute regular tap water and increase your seasoning to taste. See Basic Vegetable Stock recipe *(page 14)*.

BASIC GRAINS

Most grains can be cooked using one cup of grains and two cups of water or stock. If you prefer your grains softer, add more liquid and cook them slightly longer. For firmer grains, add less liquid.

All grains except millet benefit from presoaking and rinsing before cooking. You can soak grains for as little as one hour and as much as twenty. After that, they will start to sprout and will not require cooking. Presoaking grains washes away much of the phytic acid that hampers mineral absorption, allows them to cook faster and with less liquid, and makes them easier to assimilate and digest.

If you have the time to presoak, great. If not, don't sweat it! Just add some sea salt or a piece of kombu seaweed to the grains and continue on with the cooking. This step helps neutralize the acid-forming property of the grains and infuses them with minerals.

---

1   cup brown rice, millet, amaranth or teff
2   cups water or stock
Thumb-size piece kombu or pinch of sea salt

....

1   cup quinoa
1½ cups water or stock
Thumb-size piece kombu or pinch of sea salt

....

1   cup wild rice or whole oats
2½ cups water or stock
Thumb-size piece kombu or pinch of sea salt

Place grains in pot with enough water to cover and soak at least 1 hour. When ready to cook, pour grains into mesh basket and rinse. Return grains to pot, add fresh water or stock, kombu or salt, and bring to boil. Reduce heat to simmer, cover and cook until all liquid is absorbed. Remove from heat, discard kombu and serve.

TIPS: Cool grains slightly before fluffing so that they hold their shape and do not become mushy.

A rice cooker can be used for all grains. Presoak grains, if possible, drain, rinse and add to bowl with water or stock, and kombu or salt. Cover, turn on rice cooker and let it do its stuff!

BASIC LEGUMES

Legumes are a great source of protein that are low in fat, high in soluble fiber and iron, and boast significant health benefits. I like to make my legumes in large quantities so that I always have some prepared in my freezer. When I defrost them, I cook them minimally so that they don't split. I also keep canned legumes in my pantry as they are widely available and perfect for last minute meals. To eliminate the canned taste, pour boiling water over legumes before adding them to your recipe. I've outlined two techniques that will help you prepare dried legumes easily and without their gaseous side effects.

1　cup dried legumes
　　(pinto, kidney, aduki, black, red,
　　chickpea, cannellini…)
6　cups water or stock
Thumb-size piece kombu
Pinch of sea salt

OVERNIGHT SOAK: Place beans in pot, cover with 3 inches of water and soak overnight. When ready to cook, drain water and rinse beans.

QUICK SOAK: Rinse beans well, place in pot and cover with 3 inches of cold water. Bring almost to boil (bubbles will start to appear around edge of pot). Remove from heat, cover and let sit 1 hour. Drain water and rinse beans.

PREPARING SOAKED BEANS: Fill pot or rice cooker with 6 cups water or stock and bring to boil. Add beans and kombu and bring back to boil. Skim off and discard any foam that rises to the top of the pot. Reduce heat, add salt, cover and simmer until beans are tender. Remove from heat, drain cooking liquid and serve.

MAKES ABOUT 3 CUPS COOKED

TIP: Cook beans immediately after soaking to avoid growth of bacteria.

BASIC GREENS

There are so many different vegetables, each with its own unique nutritional profile and taste. Eating the colors of the rainbow is a great way to take full advantage of all that the vegetable kingdom has to offer. That said, I'd be taking a huge step out of character if I didn't somehow emphasize my favorites – dark leafy greens! If you can't decide how or where to begin eating clean, or even if you just need a jump-start along the way, you're always well served to turn to dark leafy greens. If they're firm and bitter, sauté them as on page 14 or add them to soups, stews, sauces or stir-fries. Try more tender greens mixed with lettuce in your salad. You'll be surprised how many different greens can be enjoyed both raw or cooked, and how great you'll feel as a result!

BASIC SAUTÉED GREENS

This recipe is perfect for dark leafy greens such as mustard greens, dandelion greens, chard, bok choy, cabbage...or my personal favorites, lacinato kale and collard greens.

1 tablespoon extra virgin olive oil
1 leek, small onion or shallot, chopped
1 garlic clove, minced
  and/or 1 tablespoon grated fresh ginger
  and/or turmeric
1 bunch or head greens, chopped
Sea salt or ume plum vinegar

In Dutch oven or large skillet over medium heat, sauté leek, onion or shallot in olive oil until soft. Add garlic and/or ginger and/or turmeric and sauté 2 minutes longer. Add greens and water a tablespoon at a time to prevent sticking and sauté until greens are tender (3–5 minutes). Remove from heat, season to taste with salt or a dash of ume plum vinegar, and serve.

BASIC VEGETABLE STOCK

My vegetable stock comes out differently every time. Sometimes I use the infused water from soaking dried shiitake mushrooms, sea vegetables or sun-dried tomatoes. Other times I save the water from steaming vegetables and use that. This recipe is delicious as is, or can be used as a template to make your own unique stock simply by adding your favorite vegetables. I also like to keep prepared vegetable stock in my pantry for backup and have found a number that are particularly clean – made from only dehydrated vegetables.

2 large yellow onions, peeled
3 large carrots
2 celery stalks
1 leek
6 garlic cloves, peeled
4–5 sprigs parsley
4–5 sprigs dill
1 bay leaf
6–8 black peppercorns
Pinch sea salt
Water

Coarsely chop onions, carrots, celery and leek and place in soup pot or large Dutch oven. Add garlic, parsley, dill, bay leaf, peppercorns and salt. Fill with enough water to cover vegetables. Bring to boil, reduce heat to simmer and cook covered for 1½ hours. Remove from heat and pour through fine-mesh basket into containers. Set aside to cool, then cover and refrigerate or freeze until ready to use.

TIPS: This stock can accommodate a variety of different vegetables and herbs, from mushrooms and celery root to shallots, fennel and thyme. I like to add the soaking water from reconstituting sea vegetables, sun-dried tomatoes and even dried fruits.

MAKING IT WORK FOR YOU

Everybody can benefit from a clean start – no matter your dietary preferences or physical needs. CLEAN START is vegan and gluten-free, so all can enjoy these recipes as they are, or take advantage of the recommendations throughout for ways to incorporate meat and dairy if you prefer. Making a clean start can be as simple as bringing in one new clean food a week, or as involved as transforming your pantry, your menus and your life.

USEFUL TIPS AND SUBSTITUTIONS

FLOUR I like to take advantage of the wide variety of savory and delicious flours when I bake. While my recipes are gluten-free, yours don't have to be. If you can't find the specific flours I've suggested, feel free to experiment with these gluten-free choices: teff flour, almond meal, sorghum, tapioca flour, brown or white rice flour. If gluten is not a concern, you can also substitute wheat and all-purpose flours. Often, retailers sell chickpea or garbanzo flour that is combined with fava bean flour. This is a perfectly good substitute.

FROZEN VEGETABLES AND FRUITS are widely available, cost-effective (even organic!) and a good alternative when you can't get fresh. You can freeze your own by washing, drying, spreading on a parchment-lined baking sheet and placing in the freezer. When firm, transfer to an airtight container and freeze until ready to use.

OILS I try to stick with oils that are cold- or expeller-pressed, unrefined and have a high heat threshold. My primary oils are extra virgin olive oil, grapeseed oil and virgin coconut oil.

SWEETENERS I use sweet fruits, citrus and vegetables to provide sweetness whenever possible. After that, I favor maple syrup, as it is minimally processed, locally grown and delicious. Less sweet options include brown rice syrup and molasses. Bringing in nutritional sweetness from fruits, vegetables and grains is a great way to reduce cravings and addictions to non-nutritional sweets.

ABOUT GLUTEN

If you are gluten intolerant or sensitive, please be aware that gluten has a way of sneaking into a variety of products. I've highlighted a few ingredients below, but it's important to always be on the lookout. Eating clean reduces your exposure to gluten, but doesn't eliminate it. Wheat, spelt, couscous, barley and rye contain gluten, so scrutinize all packaged goods for ingredients and exposure to gluten during processing. Even products that you know and love as gluten-free can be suddenly reformulated and made not gluten-free. Read every label, every time.

DRIED HERBS AND SPICES are often cut with wheat to prevent caking, and this may not be revealed on the label. Check brands online before you purchase – particularly powdered spices and packaged foods that use them, such as prepared mustard.

OATS are naturally gluten-free but become contaminated by being processed in plants that also process wheat, barley or rye. To ensure against contamination, look for certified gluten-free oats.

PASTA is traditionally a wheat/semolina product, but there are a host of non-gluten pastas widely available today made of rice, quinoa and buckwheat. If a recipe calls for pasta, select the variety best suited to your needs and preferences.

SOY SAUCE AND SHOYU are made with wheat/gluten. Tamari is traditionally wheat-free and most brands follow that guideline, but always check the ingredient list on the bottle, just in case.

Spring Dips

WHEN I WAS A CHILD, MY MOTHER USED TO MAKE DIPS that we all went crazy for. Then one day they seemed to disappear. Years later I realized that Mom had stopped making her dips when she eliminated traditional mayonnaise. When I rediscovered grapeseed oil mayonnaise, the memories of her dips came flooding back, along with my own versions of Mom's original recipes. Now I like to keep these dips on hand for easy, light and satisfying snacks.

AVOCADO DIP WITH CHIVES

2   garlic cloves, peeled
2½   avocados, peeled and pitted
½   cup grapeseed oil mayonnaise
2   tablespoons lime juice
1   tablespoon lemon juice
1   tablespoon brown rice syrup
¼   teaspoon sea salt
¼   cup chopped fresh chives

With food processor running, drop in garlic and process until minced. Turn off processor, scrape down sides, add avocados and purée until smooth. Add mayonnaise, lime juice, lemon juice, brown rice syrup and salt, and purée until smooth. Add most of the chives, leaving out just a few for garnish, and process briefly to combine. Adjust seasoning to taste, and serve topped with remaining chopped chives.

MAKES 1½ cups

VARIATIONS
Add a little spice to this dip with a few dashes of hot sauce or a teaspoon of wasabi powder.

SERVING SUGGESTIONS
This dip goes great with crudités such as carrots, celery, daikon, jícama and radishes. It's also a great spread for a roasted tofu or veggie sandwich, or wrapped in nori with salmon, cucumber and sprouts.

CURRY DIP

2   garlic cloves, peeled
1   cup grapeseed oil mayonnaise
1   tablespoon brown rice vinegar
1½   teaspoons curry powder
¼   teaspoon ground turmeric
¼   teaspoon ground coriander
¼   teaspoon ground cumin
¼   teaspoon grated fresh ginger
¼   teaspoon sea salt

With food processor running, drop in garlic and process until minced. Turn processor off and add remaining ingredients. Process on pulse to combine and serve. Dip can be stored for up to 3 days in airtight container in refrigerator.

MAKES 1 cup

Spicy Black Bean Dip

I'M A NUT FOR BLACK BEANS. In the summer I toss them with vegetables, herbs and lime juice. In the winter, they're perfect in warming soups and chilis. And in the spring (and also in the fall!) I serve this savory and spicy dip as a snack or appetizer with corn chips, and even use it as a base for tacos or burritos. My family devours it either way, and always comes back looking for more.

1	garlic clove, minced
3	tablespoons chopped red onion
3	tablespoons extra virgin olive oil
2	tablespoons chopped chiles (any variety)
⅛	teaspoon chile powder
1½	cups cooked black beans
1	tablespoon plus 1 teaspoon tomato paste
½	teaspoon sea salt

In small skillet over medium heat, sauté garlic and onion in 1½ tablespoons olive oil until soft (about 3 minutes). Add chiles and chile powder and remove from heat.

Place black beans in food processor and pulse to chop. Add onion mixture, tomato paste, salt and remaining 1½ tablespoons oil. Pulse to combine and continue processing until desired texture is achieved. Serve at room temperature or refrigerate to chill.

MAKES 1½ cups

TIPS
Select chile variety based on desired heat/spice.

SERVING SUGGESTIONS
This recipe can be doubled or even tripled easily. If you make extra, you'll have plenty to serve as a dip, plus leftovers to use as filling for tacos, burritos or enchiladas.

Roasted Cauliflower and Garlic Soup

CAULIFLOWER NEVER THRILLED ME MUCH UNTIL I realized what a great base it made for creamy soups and sauces. Roasting cauliflower brings out its unique flavor. That's all it took to turn me into a convert! Add some roasted garlic and you just can't go wrong.

2	heads cauliflower (about 10 cups chopped)
4	tablespoons extra virgin olive oil, plus extra for rubbing garlic
1	garlic bulb
1	cup diced sweet onion (try cipollini or Vidalia)
2	tablespoons mirin
2	teaspoons sea salt
4	cups vegetable stock or water
2	tablespoons fresh thyme leaves
	Ground white pepper

Preheat oven to 350°F.

Place cauliflower in 9 x 13-inch baking dish, drizzle with 2 tablespoons olive oil and toss to coat. Cut off top of garlic, rub entire bulb with oil and wrap in foil. Place both in oven and roast for about 1 hour or until soft, tossing cauliflower occasionally. Remove from oven and set aside. When garlic is cool enough to handle, separate cloves, peel and discard skins and set aside.

In soup pot or large Dutch oven over medium-low heat, sauté onion in 1 tablespoon olive oil until translucent (about 5 minutes). Add roasted cauliflower and garlic, mirin, salt and stock or water, increase heat and bring to boil. Reduce heat and simmer 5 minutes. Remove from heat and purée until smooth with handheld blender. Return to heat, stir in 1 tablespoon thyme and pepper, and simmer 20 minutes to allow flavors to blend. Remove from heat and stir in remaining tablespoon oil, garnish with remaining thyme leaves and serve.

SERVES 6

SERVING SUGGESTION
Frizzled leeks make a great condiment for this soup. Thinly slice leeks, sauté in olive oil until bright green then spread on parchment-lined cookie sheet and bake at 350°F until crisp.

Creamy Split Pea Soup with Meyer Lemon Zest and Thyme

MY LOCAL NATURAL FOOD STORE has an incredible selection of prepared foods, yet I always end up selecting the split pea soup. While I love making my own, it's so comforting to know that this soup is always there prepared and waiting for me. No matter where I am in my day, I find it a calming and soothing treat. This version is perked up with the addition of sweet and tart Meyer lemons. It freezes well, so make enough to put some away for another day.

---

1   large onion, diced
3   stalks celery, diced
1   tablespoon grapeseed oil
3   tablespoons fresh thyme leaves
3   tablespoons mirin
Sea salt
White pepper
3   cups green split peas
10 cups vegetable stock
1   Meyer lemon (zest and juice)

In soup pot or large Dutch oven over medium heat, sauté onion and celery in oil until soft (about 4 minutes). Add thyme and mirin, season generously with salt and white pepper and sauté 2 minutes longer.

Rinse split peas and add to pot with sautéed vegetables. Add stock and bring to boil. Reduce heat to simmer, cover and cook for 2½ hours or until peas are soft and soup is thick. If peas don't fall apart completely, purée with handheld blender until smooth. Remove from heat, stir in lemon juice and season to taste with salt and pepper. Top with lemon zest and serve.

SERVES 6

Kale, Sweet Potato and White Bean Soup

I'D LIKE TO BE ABLE TO SAY that I always take my time and mindfully prepare meals for my family, but sometimes it's just not reality. Often, by the time I get around to meal preparation, it's nearly time to eat. This soup is the answer. Put what you have in a pot, add stock and while it cooks, set the table and clean the kitchen. The ingredients are so basic, I fall back on this recipe often when time's running short.

1   small yellow onion, diced

2   tablespoons grated
    fresh ginger

1   tablespoon
    extra virgin olive oil

3   stalks celery, diced

1   large sweet potato,
    peeled and diced

3   cups cooked great
    northern or navy beans,
    rinsed

3   tablespoons mirin

1   bunch kale, chopped

Vegetable stock

Pinch of ground nutmeg

Sea salt and freshly ground
    black pepper

Gomasio or toasted
    sesame seeds

In soup pot or large Dutch oven over medium heat, sauté onion and ginger in olive oil until soft (about 3 minutes). Add celery, sweet potato, beans and mirin, and stir. Add kale and enough vegetable stock to cover all ingredients by an inch. Bring to boil, reduce heat, cover and simmer for 30 minutes to cook potatoes through and allow flavors to develop. Season to taste with nutmeg, salt and pepper, and serve topped with gomasio or toasted sesame seeds.

SERVES 4

Arame Sauté

IF YOU'RE NEW TO COOKING WITH SEA VEGETABLES, arame is a great place to start, as it has a mild flavor and requires only a short soaking time to reconstitute. This dish can be served fresh off the stove, at room temperature or chilled. Try it with a piece of grilled fish, vegetable nori rolls or some marinated and grilled tofu or tempeh.

½ cup dried arame

3 cups hot water

½ cup thinly sliced red onion

1 teaspoon grapeseed oil

1 cup julienned carrots

1 cup peeled and julienned broccoli stems

1 cup julienned daikon

2 tablespoons mirin

1 tablespoon toasted sesame seeds

DRESSING

2 tablespoons brown rice syrup

1 tablespoon whole grain mustard

½ teaspoon apple cider vinegar

¼ teaspoon ume plum vinegar

Soak arame in hot water for 20 minutes. Drain well, coarsely chop and set aside.

In large skillet over medium heat, sauté onion in oil for 2 minutes to soften slightly. Add carrots, broccoli stems, daikon and mirin, and sauté 3–5 minutes or until vegetables are soft. Fold in arame.

In separate bowl, whisk together all dressing ingredients. Pour over vegetables and sauté 1 minute longer to combine and heat through. Stir in sesame seeds, remove from heat and serve.

SERVES 4

Watercress and Fennel Salad with Blood Orange and Thyme Vinaigrette

THE COMBINATION OF BITTER GREENS, soothing fennel and tart blood orange makes this a super-refreshing and beautiful addition to nearly any spring menu. For a completely different taste, substitute fresh mint leaves for the thyme, or use both!

2   blood oranges

2   bunches watercress, trimmed

½   fennel bulb, cored and thinly sliced

VINAIGRETTE

¼   cup lemon juice

¼   teaspoon lemon zest

½   cup extra virgin olive oil

1   tablespoon minced shallot

4   teaspoons maple syrup

1   tablespoon fresh thyme leaves, chopped

Sea salt and freshly ground black pepper

To prepare oranges, cut off both ends, and cut between the peel and the orange to remove peel and pith completely. Cut oranges crosswise into ¼-inch slices, place in bowl and set aside.

Arrange watercress on individual plates or on a large platter and top with sliced fennel.

In small bowl, whisk together lemon juice, lemon zest, olive oil, shallot, maple syrup and thyme leaves. Season to taste with salt and pepper. Remove oranges from bowl and arrange on salad. Pour remaining juice from oranges into the vinaigrette bowl. Whisk to combine, drizzle evenly over salad and serve.

SERVES 4

Mixed Spring Greens with Currants and Pepitas

MY FAVORITE GREETING CARD OF ALL TIME shows mother and child dinosaurs around a kitchen table. The mother says, "Eat your greens or you'll go extinct!" I'm thinking of making that my mantra. If you're not accustomed to eating bitter greens, try the baby greens of spring as they're less bitter and offer an easy place to start. Add some sweet currants and salty pumpkin seeds and you'll be enjoying greens like you never thought you could.

¼   cup minced red onion

2   garlic cloves, minced

1   tablespoon
extra virgin olive oil

¼   cup currants

1   teaspoon chopped
fresh rosemary

1   tablespoon mirin

1   head escarole, chopped
into bite-size pieces

3   baby bok choy, chopped
into bite-size pieces

1   small radicchio, chopped
into bite-size pieces

Freshly ground black pepper

4–5 dashes ume plum vinegar

¼   cup toasted
pepitas/pumpkin seeds
(salted or unsalted)

In large skillet over medium heat, sauté onion and garlic in olive oil until soft (about 3 minutes). Add currants, rosemary and mirin and sauté 1 minute longer. Fold in escarole, bok choy and radicchio and sauté until leaves are bright and just starting to wilt. Remove from heat and season to taste with pepper and ume plum vinegar. Fold in half of the pepitas and serve topped with remaining pepitas.

SERVES 4

VARIATION
Add some heat to this dish by substituting crushed red pepper flakes for the black pepper.

TIP
This dish is best prepared just before serving, as the greens will continue to wilt after they've been prepared.

Raw Kale Confetti Salad with Toasted Sunflower Seeds

THIS LIGHT AND RAW PREPARATION OF KALE is the perfect warm-weather alternative to sautéing and allows me to keep the nutritional powerhouse of kale in my diet year-round. If you thought kale required cooking, you'll be delightfully surprised at how tender and delicious this preparation is.

---

2   bunches kale (about 4 heaping cups chopped)

2   tablespoons extra virgin olive oil

⅛   teaspoon sea salt, plus more to taste

1   teaspoon grated fresh ginger

½   avocado, peeled, pitted and chopped

3   tablespoons finely chopped red onion

3   tablespoons finely chopped red bell pepper

1   small carrot, grated

3   tablespoons toasted sunflower seeds

1   tablespoon lemon juice

1   tablespoon lime juice

Remove stalks from kale and discard. Chop leaves into small pieces and place in mixing bowl. Drizzle with olive oil and, using your fingers, gently massage oil into leaves. Sprinkle with sea salt and ginger, add avocado and continue massaging until leaves are evenly coated. Set aside to marinate for 15 minutes.

Add onion, red pepper, carrot and sunflower seeds, and toss. Drizzle lemon and lime juice over salad, massage juices into leaves and toss to distribute ingredients evenly. Season to taste with salt, massage one last time and serve.

SERVES 4

VARIATIONS
Try this raw kale salad with fresh basil, heirloom tomatoes and avocado in the summer, or red onion, orange slices and pumpkin seeds in winter.

Asparagus with Miso Lemon Dressing and Marcona Almonds

MISO IS A GREAT SOURCE of essential vitamin B$_{12}$ and immune-strengthening zinc. Plus, it delivers big taste and significant health benefits. In the winter, it's easy to add miso to soups and stews. Come spring, I favor lighter preparations like this one that contrast miso's taste with the delicate and sweet Marcona almonds and fresh asparagus to highlight the flavors of the season.

2	bunches asparagus
¼	cup water
3	garlic cloves, minced
2	tablespoons extra virgin olive oil
2	tablespoons lemon juice
1	tablespoon sweet brown rice miso
¼	cup Marcona almonds (or whole blanched almonds)

To prepare asparagus, cut off and discard woody ends and chop remaining stalks into bite-size pieces.

In large skillet or Dutch oven over high heat, bring water to boil. Add asparagus and cook 2 minutes or until bright green and just soft. Remove from heat, drain water and set aside.

In small skillet over medium-low heat, sauté garlic in olive oil until soft (about 3 minutes). Remove from heat and stir in lemon juice and miso, mixing until miso is dissolved. Pour dressing over asparagus, transfer to serving dish, top with almonds and serve.

SERVES 4

Seared Artichokes with Lemon and Capers

MY MOTHER USED TO MAKE THE MOST INCREDIBLE stuffed artichokes. Now that I'm a mother, I don't have the time or waistline to afford such a luxury! Instead, I make my artichokes with this light and lemony dressing that requires a fraction of the prep time and has just as much taste as Mom's.

2   artichokes

Lemon juice

¼   cup capers

Sea salt and freshly ground black pepper

2   tablespoons chopped fresh flat-leaf parsley or cilantro

Chopped fresh chives

DRESSING

¼   cup extra virgin olive oil

2   garlic cloves, minced

¼   cup lemon juice

¼   cup white wine

Prepare artichokes by removing tough lower leaves and peeling stem. Cut off and discard top ½ inch of artichokes where leaves are tight. Snip off sharp points from remaining leaves and cut artichokes in half, from stem to tip. Cut out fuzzy chokes, slice each artichoke half into thirds, and rub all cut surfaces with lemon juice. Fill large pot or Dutch oven with 4 inches of water and bring to boil. Place artichokes in boiling water and cook until leaves and hearts are soft. Remove from heat and drain well.

In small bowl, whisk together olive oil, garlic, lemon juice and white wine. In large skillet over high heat, pour in 2 tablespoons of dressing to coat bottom of pan. Place artichokes side by side in pan and top with capers. Sauté for 4–5 minutes per side, adding dressing a little at a time to prevent burning and to season chokes. When all dressing has been used and artichokes are evenly seared on both sides, remove from heat and season to taste with salt and pepper. Fold in parsley or cilantro, top with chives and serve.

SERVES 4

Cannellini Beans with Sun-Dried Tomatoes and Ramps

RAMPS ARE WILD LEEKS that are harvested in early spring. Their taste combines the flavors of garlic and scallion and can be quite strong…and quite delicious! This recipe highlights their earthy pungency, in contrast to the rich and creamy beans and sweet and salty sun-dried tomatoes for a result that's sure to satisfy.

8	sun-dried tomatoes
½	cup water
12	ramps
1	tablespoons extra virgin olive oil
1	tablespoon mirin
3	cups cooked cannellini beans
Sea salt and freshly ground black pepper	

Place sun-dried tomatoes in small bowl. Bring water to boil, pour over tomatoes and set aside for 15 minutes or until soft. Remove tomatoes from bowl and save soaking water. Mince tomatoes and set aside.

Wash ramps, cut off and discard root ends and chop bulbs and greens into thin slices. In large skillet over medium heat, sauté tomatoes in olive oil for 3 minutes. Add ramps and mirin and continue sautéing for 2 minutes. Add liquid from reconstituting tomatoes 1 tablespoon at a time as needed to prevent sticking. Add beans and 2 tablespoons more of the tomato liquid. Continue cooking until beans are heated through and there is almost no liquid remaining in pan. Season to taste with salt and pepper, remove from heat and serve.

SERVES 4

TIP
Cannellini beans are super-soft and creamy, but I also like to make this recipe with fava beans.

SERVING SUGGESTIONS
My favorite way to enjoy these beans is spooned over a thick slice of oiled and grilled sourdough bread, but they're also great tossed with penne pasta, over grilled polenta or used as a base for a seafood stew.

Maple Mustard and Tahini Glazed Carrots

THE MULTICOLORED BABY CARROTS available in late spring in eye-catching reds, whites, purples and yes, even traditional orange, are the perfect size, super-sweet and impossible to pass by. These are *not* the machine-cut and prepackaged ones! If baby carrots aren't available, you're sure to love this recipe even if you use regular carrots cut into sticks or rounds.

1 pound baby carrots

Sea salt

2 tablespoons maple syrup

1 tablespoon whole grain mustard

1 teaspoon tahini

1 teaspoon lemon juice

Wash carrots and trim leafy greens, leaving about ½ inch of their stems. Fill large sauté pan with 1 inch of water and bring to boil. Stir in generous pinch of salt and place carrots side by side in water. Cook until just soft and water is nearly evaporated (about 6 minutes, depending on size of carrots). Remove from heat, drain remaining water and set aside.

In small pan over medium heat, whisk together maple syrup, mustard, tahini and lemon juice. Season to taste with salt and remove from heat.

Return carrots in skillet to medium heat and add maple mustard dressing. Sauté 1–2 minutes to coat carrots and heat through. Dressing will thicken slightly. Remove from heat and serve.

SERVES 4

VARIATION
Slice your carrots into rings and mix with sliced parsnip. For an even bigger change, substitute grated fresh horseradish root for the tahini.

Polenta Pizzas

AMONG THE MANY GLUTEN-FREE PEOPLE I MEET, almost all say they miss pizza more than any other food. This version is sure to please those who are gluten-free as well as those who are not. The crust can be made hours in advance. Keep it wrapped and refrigerated, and bake it when you make your topping of choice.

POLENTA PIZZA CRUST

3	cups vegetable stock
1	teaspoon sea salt
½	teaspoon dried basil
½	teaspoon dried oregano
½	teaspoon dried parsley

Freshly ground black pepper

2	tablespoons extra virgin olive oil
1¼	cups polenta

Cornmeal

KALE AND MAITAKE MUSHROOM TOPPING

1	large leek, sliced
3	tablespoons extra virgin olive oil
3	tablespoons mirin
2	maitake mushrooms
1	bunch kale, finely chopped

Sea salt and black pepper

¼	cup pasta sauce

CHARD AND PARSLEY PESTO TOPPING

½	small red onion, thinly sliced
3	garlic cloves
3	tablespoons extra virgin olive oil
1	bunch Swiss chard, chopped

Sea salt and black pepper

¼	cup Parsley Walnut Pesto *(page 100)*

PREPARING CRUST

Over high heat, bring stock to boil. Reduce heat to medium and add salt, basil, oregano, parsley, pepper and olive oil. Whisking continuously, pour in polenta and continue whisking for 5–7 minutes until smooth and thick. Pour into two 11-inch tart pans and spread evenly over bottom of each pan. Cool slightly and then refrigerate for 30 minutes or until firm.

Preheat oven to 350°F and place pizza stone or baking sheet on middle rack. Remove polenta from refrigerator, sprinkle pizza stone or baking sheet with cornmeal, transfer polenta to stone or baking sheet and bake 40 minutes. Remove from oven and set aside.

PREPARING TOPPINGS

For kale pizza, place large skillet over medium heat and sauté leek in 1½ tablespoons olive oil for 3 minutes. Add mirin and sauté 2 minutes longer. Crumble maitake mushrooms, add to pan and sauté 5 minutes or until soft. Fold in kale and sauté 3 minutes longer. Drizzle with remaining olive oil, season to taste with salt and black pepper and remove from heat.

For chard pizza, sauté onion and garlic in oil until soft, following the directions for the kale topping. Add chard, sauté 1 minute, remove from heat, and season to taste with salt and pepper.

Spread pasta sauce or parsley pesto evenly over crust, leaving a ½-inch edge. Top with kale or chard mixture and return to oven to bake 15 minutes. Remove from oven, cut with pizza wheel and serve.

MAKES two 10-inch pizzas

VARIATION
If you're short on time, brown-rice tortillas make a great last-minute pizza crust.

Asian Spinach with Peanut Ginger Sauce

THIS DISH IS INSPIRED by the Japanese staple spinach gomae – spinach with sesame. Traditionally served cold in a pool of sauce, it tastes equally delicious warm. Tender baby spinach is one of the first greens to appear in the greenhouses each spring, when my mind and body are still in cooked greens mode. This recipe deliciously bridges the gap to warmer weather and more cooling preparations.

---

8 cups firmly packed chopped fresh spinach

3 tablespoons peanut butter

2 teaspoons grated fresh ginger

1 teaspoon tamari

1 teaspoon maple syrup

½ teaspoon toasted sesame oil or hot sesame oil

3 tablespoons hot water

2 tablespoons chopped roasted peanuts

Fill large skillet or Dutch oven with ¼ inch of water and bring to boil. Add spinach and water-sauté until just wilted. Time will vary according to maturity and variety of spinach, but expect 30 seconds to 2 minutes at most. Remove from heat and set aside.

In bowl, whisk together peanut butter, ginger, tamari, maple syrup, sesame oil and hot water. Drain spinach and squeeze to remove excess water. Place in serving dish, drizzle sauce over top, finish with chopped peanuts and serve.

SERVES 4

VARIATIONS
If you're allergic to nuts, substitute sunflower butter and toasted sunflower seeds for the peanut butter and peanuts.

Sweet Brown Rice with Leeks, Ginger and Garlic

OFTEN WHEN PLANNING A MEAL, I opt for the most basic preparation for whole grains so that they can blend with and highlight a variety of dishes and flavors. Other times, I prefer to amp up the taste and textures of my basic recipe, as I've done here. This is a perfect dish to accompany Baby Bok Choy with Hot Sesame Oil and Lime *(page 44),* or sautéed kale or collard greens.

1¼ cups sweet brown rice

2½ cups water or vegetable stock

Thumb-size piece kombu

1 large leek, finely chopped

3 tablespoons grated fresh ginger

5 large garlic cloves, minced

2 tablespoons extra virgin olive oil

1 tablespoon mirin

½ cup toasted pumpkin seeds (salted or unsalted)

Rinse rice and place in pot with water or stock and kombu. Bring to boil, reduce heat, cover and simmer 25 minutes or until liquid is absorbed. Remove from heat and set aside to cool slightly.

In Dutch oven over medium heat, sauté leeks, ginger and garlic in oil for 2–3 minutes. Add mirin and continue sautéing until leek is soft. Remove from heat and set aside.

Remove kombu from rice and discard. Fluff rice with fork, then fold into sautéed leek mixture. Return pan to heat and sauté to combine ingredients and heat through (add water 1 tablespoon at a time to deglaze pan as needed). Top with toasted pumpkin seeds and serve.

SERVES 4

Chickpea, Avocado and Pea Shoot Salad with Orange Dill Dressing

THIS HIGH-PROTEIN SALAD is every bit as hearty and satisfying as it is light and refreshing. Serving it warm allows the flavors to stand out, and brings out the richness of the avocado. Pea shoots can be hard to come by and won't make or break your salad. They're well worth a bit of searching, as they're nutrient-packed, tender and delicious, but if you can't find them, you'll enjoy this combination equally well with watercress.

½   small red onion, minced

1   large carrot, finely chopped

2–3 red radishes, thinly sliced

1½ cups cooked chickpeas

4   cups water

½   red bell pepper, finely chopped

2   avocados, peeled, pitted and diced

1   cup pea shoots, washed

DRESSING

1   tablespoon extra virgin olive oil

1   tablespoon balsamic vinegar

2   tablespoons freshly squeezed orange juice

Zest of 1 orange

1   tablespoon lime juice

1   tablespoon chopped fresh dill

Sea salt and freshly ground black pepper

Place onion, carrot, radishes and chickpeas in large bowl. Bring water to boil and pour over vegetables. Let sit 2–3 minutes to soften vegetables. Drain water well and set aside.

In small skillet over medium heat, prepare dressing by whisking together olive oil, vinegar, orange juice and zest, lime juice and dill. Season to taste with salt and pepper and simmer until heated through.

Add red pepper, avocados and pea shoots to salad and drizzle dressing evenly over top. Toss to coat and serve warm.

SERVES 4

Baby Bok Choy with Hot Sesame Oil and Lime

BOK CHOY IS ALWAYS A WELCOME ADDITION to stir-fries or salads, but these individual baby cabbages are so bright green and beautiful that I like to showcase them in their entirety. Dirt can collect down near the root end, so gently bend the stalks out, away from the root end, and wash out nooks and crannies.

4–5 heads baby bok choy

1 tablespoon grapeseed oil

1 tablespoon lime juice

1 teaspoon hot sesame oil

1 teaspoon toasted sesame oil

¼ teaspoon ume plum vinegar

1 teaspoon toasted black sesame seeds

1 teaspoon toasted ivory sesame seeds

Keep smaller bok choy heads whole and slice larger ones in half the long way. Wash well and trim off dried root ends. Place steaming rack in pot over 2 inches water, bring to boil, add bok choy and steam 3 minutes or until just bright green (time will vary according to size of bok choy). Remove from heat and place bok choy on platter or individual plates.

In small bowl, whisk together grapeseed oil, lime juice, hot sesame oil, toasted sesame oil and ume plum vinegar. Pour over bok choy, top with sesame seeds and serve.

SERVES 4

TIPS

For extra heat, use more hot sesame oil and less toasted sesame oil, and vice versa for less heat. As an alternative to sesame altogether, sauté 2 cloves minced garlic and 1 minced shallot in olive oil, stir in a dash of lime juice and use that as your dressing.

Seared Tempeh with Dried Cherries and Pine Nuts over Arugula

THERE ARE A FEW OF US IN MY FAMILY who adore tempeh, and the rest are in denial. I can serve it to rave reviews, but as soon as they realize it's tempeh, they change their minds. Rather than fight it, I simply make most of my tempeh dishes for my own lunchtime enjoyment. This recipe is one of those lunchtime treats, but it can easily be served as a one-dish dinner, too! To achieve an evenly browned tempeh, I suggest a cast-iron skillet.

8	ounces tempeh
¼	cup chopped red onion
1	tablespoon extra virgin olive oil
½	cup chopped dried cherries
1	tablespoon mirin
2	tablespoons lemon juice
4	cups fresh arugula
½	cup toasted pine nuts

VINAIGRETTE

1	tablespoon balsamic vinegar
2	tablespoons lemon juice
3	tablespoons extra virgin olive oil

Zest of 1 orange

Sea salt and freshly ground black pepper

Slice tempeh into ¼-inch strips and steam for 5 minutes. Remove from heat and set aside. Whisk together vinaigrette ingredients and set aside.

In large cast-iron skillet over medium heat, sauté onion in olive oil for 2 minutes. Stir in cherries, mirin and 1 tablespoon lemon juice. Place tempeh strips side by side in pan and sauté 2 minutes. Drizzle 1 tablespoon of the vinaigrette over tempeh and continue sautéing 2 minutes longer. Flip tempeh and deglaze pan with remaining tablespoon lemon juice. Sauté 2 minutes, then drizzle tempeh with another tablespoon of vinaigrette. When both sides of tempeh are evenly browned, remove from heat and set aside.

Place arugula in mixing bowl and toss with remaining vinaigrette. Transfer to serving dish, top with seared tempeh and cherries, sprinkle with pine nuts and serve.

SERVES 4

Festive Quinoa with Apricots and Orange Zest

I HAD BEEN ENJOYING IVORY QUINOA FOR YEARS before I discovered Inca red quinoa, with its appealing burnt-red color and mellow taste that complement a variety of dishes. Serve this dish with everything from Roasted Cauliflower and Garlic Soup *(page 23)* to Asparagus with Miso Lemon Dressing and Marcona Almonds *(page 32)* and even just a simple green salad.

1½ cups Inca red quinoa

2¾ cups water

Sea salt

½ cup dried apricots

½ fennel bulb, cored and diced

1 bunch scallions, chopped

1 cup toasted pine nuts

½ cup chopped fresh basil

¼ cup chopped fresh mint

2 tablespoons orange zest

¼ cup extra virgin olive oil

1 tablespoon maple syrup

Juice and zest of 1 lemon

Freshly ground black pepper

2 tablespoons toasted sesame seeds

Place quinoa in pot or rice cooker with water and pinch of salt. Bring to boil, reduce heat, and simmer covered until liquid is absorbed (about 15 minutes). Remove from heat and set aside to cool slightly before fluffing.

Place apricots in bowl. Bring 1 cup water to boil and pour over apricots to reconstitute. Let sit 1 minute, drain and chop. Transfer to large mixing bowl and add fennel, scallions and pine nuts. Fluff quinoa and add to bowl.

In small bowl, whisk together basil, mint, orange zest, olive oil, maple syrup and lemon juice and zest. Season to taste with salt and pepper and pour over quinoa mixture. Add toasted sesame seeds, fold to combine all ingredients and serve.

SERVES 6

Chewy Chocolate Macaroons

I ADORE MACAROONS and make them in huge batches – doubling and even tripling the recipe each time! These freeze well, so you can have a supply on hand for unexpected guests or just for sneaking a few when cravings arise. Not that I ever do that, but I'm just saying...

2 cups shredded unsweetened coconut

¼ teaspoon sea salt

¼ cup coconut milk

¼ cup maple syrup

1 teaspoon almond extract

1 cup gluten- and dairy-free chocolate chips or 6 ounces dark chocolate

Preheat oven to 350°F.

In large mixing bowl, combine coconut with salt. In separate bowl, whisk together coconut milk, maple syrup and almond extract. Add to coconut and stir until evenly moist.

Melt chocolate chips or chocolate in double boiler or in small pot over very low heat and pour into coconut mixture. Fold until evenly combined. Line cookie sheet with parchment paper. Scoop batter by the tablespoonful and place on cookie sheet in equal-size mounds. Gently press to make each mound of mixture stick together. Bake 18–20 minutes or until tops appear dry. Remove from heat and place on rack to cool.

MAKES 18 macaroons

Banana Date Cake

AFTER YEARS OF MAKING BANANA BREAD with my mother's tried-and-true recipe made with wheat flour, I assumed there was no way that a gluten-free variation was going to live up to my expectations. I was wrong. This banana date cake has become so popular in my home that my children let the bananas get overripe just so I'll make it.

WET INGREDIENTS

10	dried dates, pitted
2	ripe bananas
⅓	cup maple syrup
¼	cup virgin coconut oil, melted
2	tablespoons lemon juice
1	teaspoon vanilla extract

DRY INGREDIENTS

1	cup chickpea flour
1	cup almond meal
¼	cup tapioca flour
1	tablespoon baking powder
1	teaspoon baking soda
½	teaspoon ground cinnamon
½	teaspoon sea salt

Preheat oven to 350°F and lightly grease 8 x 8-inch glass baking dish.

Place dates in large bowl and cover with boiling water to soften. Drain well, add bananas and mash both together so that chunks remain. Add maple syrup, melted oil, lemon juice and vanilla and whisk to combine.

In separate bowl, whisk together all dry ingredients. Add to bowl with banana mixture and fold gently to combine, making sure not to over-mix. Pour into prepared baking dish and bake for 30 minutes or until toothpick inserted in center comes out clean. Remove from oven, place on rack and cool completely before slicing or removing from dish.

MAKES 1 cake

VARIATION
Drizzle melted chocolate over the top for an extra-special presentation.

Rhubarb Cream with Strawberries and Candied Ginger

IT'S HARD TO GO WRONG with these late-spring ingredients. I like to serve this dish in individual parfait or martini glasses, but my children are just as happy to get it in any old bowl, as long as Mom doesn't devour it before it gets to the table! If you don't care for candied ginger, top your parfait with strawberries and granola.

5 cups chopped rhubarb

Juice and zest of 1 orange

1 cup maple syrup

1 tablespoon arrowroot, dissolved in 2 tablespoons water

1 teaspoon vanilla extract

2 pounds firm silken tofu

½ cup chopped candied ginger

1 pound strawberries, hulled and sliced

Place rhubarb in medium pot over medium heat. Add orange juice and maple syrup, stir to combine and bring to boil. Reduce heat, cover and simmer 6 minutes or until rhubarb starts to fall apart. Stir in dissolved arrowroot and continue stirring until mixture thickens (about 2 minutes). Remove from heat, stir in vanilla and set aside.

Wrap tofu in towels and press to remove excess water. Place in food processor and process until smooth. Scrape down sides of bowl and pulse briefly to whip all tofu. Add slightly cooled rhubarb mixture and pulse gently to combine. Remove bowl from food processor, cover and refrigerate 1 hour or until cool.

To assemble, combine candied ginger and orange zest in separate bowl. Spoon rhubarb cream into serving glasses, top with strawberries and candied ginger/zest combination and serve.

SERVES 4

Summer Salsas

THE GREEN GODDESS, IN MY FIRST BOOK, was a delightfully mellow and creamy dip featuring fresh herbs. The Grilled Salsa Verde here is its alter ego, with a bold flavor and plenty of kick. Contrast that with the tangy, sweet and refreshing Tomatillo and Yellow Plum Salsa, and you have salsas for all occasions.

TOMATILLO AND YELLOW PLUM SALSA

8	tomatillos, husked and chopped
4	yellow plums, pitted and chopped
½	green bell pepper, minced
½	small red onion, minced
12	cherry tomatoes, chopped
1	jalapeño, seeded and minced
1	garlic clove, minced
¼	cup chopped fresh cilantro
1	tablespoon extra virgin olive oil
1	tablespoon lime juice

Sea salt and freshly ground black pepper

In medium bowl, combine tomatillos, plums, bell pepper, onion, tomatoes, jalapeño, garlic and cilantro. Drizzle with olive oil and lime juice and stir to combine all ingredients. Season to taste with salt and pepper and serve.

MAKES 1½–2 cups (depending on size of fruit)

VARIATIONS

If the season for yellow plums has passed, substitute 1 cup finely chopped honeydew or cantaloupe.

GRILLED SALSA VERDE

6	tomatillos, husked and halved
2	poblano chiles, stemmed, halved and seeded
½	small yellow onion
½	cup packed fresh cilantro leaves
2	tablespoons lime juice

Splash of extra virgin olive oil

Sea salt

Preheat grill to medium.

Place tomatillos face down on grill rack along with chiles and onion. Grill 5–6 minutes and flip. Grill 5–6 minutes longer or until onion and chiles are mostly cooked and tomatillo juice starts to bubble over. Remove from grill, and peel off and discard any charred areas of skin. Place in food processor with cilantro and lime juice. Process to mince and combine. Season to taste with olive oil and salt, and serve.

MAKES 1½ cups

VARIATIONS

This salsa can be made raw simply by combining all ingredients in food processor. For added sweetness, add green tomatoes to the mix. For extra heat, add a jalapeño or serrano chile, stemmed and seeded.

Zesty Jícama

A BOX GRATER AND FIVE MINUTES IS ALL IT TAKES to make this refreshing cross between a slaw and a salsa. While I initially created this recipe as a salsa to serve with corn chips, I quickly realized that it was equally delicious as a topping for sliced heirloom tomatoes, gazpacho and even Bloody Marys! However you use it, it's sure to add zest to your summer menus.

---

3   cups peeled and coarsely grated jícama

⅓   cup plus 2 tablespoons minced fresh cilantro

2   tablespoons minced fresh mint

2   teaspoons grated fresh ginger

2   tablespoons lemon juice

2   tablespoons lime juice

Zest of 1 lime

¼   teaspoon sea salt

In medium mixing bowl, combine jícama, cilantro and mint. In separate bowl, whisk together ginger, lemon juice, lime juice and zest and salt. Pour over slaw, toss to combine and serve.

SERVES 4

VARIATIONS
Experiment with a variety of summer herbs from orange or pineapple mint to lemon balm and even purple, cinnamon or Thai basil.

Chilled Chickpea, Tomatillo and Avocado Soup

EVERY RULE HAS ITS EXCEPTION, and creating this recipe taught me an important one. Sometimes, it really is best to wait until a recipe is done before you taste! If you end up sneaking a taste early on, rest assured, the flavors will mellow and blend beautifully once the soup has chilled. In the end, your chilled soup will be creamy, light and refreshing, and a great starter for your summer barbeque.

4	tomatillos, husked
2	garlic cloves, minced
¼	cup finely chopped sweet onion
2	tablespoons extra virgin olive oil, plus more for drizzling
1	tablespoon mirin
3	cups cooked chickpeas
3	avocados, peeled, pitted and chopped
¼	cup lime juice
3	cups water
¾	teaspoon sea salt
½	cup fresh basil leaves
2	tablespoons chopped fresh chives
¼	cup chopped cherry tomatoes

Bring 2-quart pot of water to boil. Score bottom of each tomatillo with a small "x" and place in boiling water. Cook 3 minutes, drain cooking water and rinse with cold water. Set aside to cool.

In soup pot or large Dutch oven over medium-high heat, sauté garlic and onion in olive oil until soft (about 3 minutes). Add mirin, chickpeas, avocados, lime juice and water. When tomatillos are cool enough to touch, peel away thick outside skin, chop fruit and add to soup. Add salt, bring soup to boil, reduce heat and simmer 15 minutes. Remove from heat and purée with handheld blender until smooth. Stir in basil leaves and purée on pulse to chop and incorporate into soup. Stir in chives and return to heat to simmer 5 minutes longer. Remove from heat and set aside. When soup is room temperature, cover and refrigerate 1 hour. When ready to serve, top with chopped cherry tomatoes and an extra drizzle of olive oil.

SERVES 4

VARIATION
Serve topped with mint leaves, grated jícama, grilled shrimp and/or a dash of Old Bay!

Peach Gazpacho
with Heirloom Tomatoes

FROM MY CHILDHOOD, I remember only three kinds of tomatoes – cherry, plum and beefsteak. Now I taste my way through each summer, enjoying dozens of varieties of tomatoes, each one unique and delicious. My two favorite varieties are the garden peach and the strawberry husk tomatoes, and I like to combine them with super-sweet cherry tomatoes when I make this refreshing soup. A visit to the farmers market and a food processor will have you enjoying this sweet gazpacho in no time.

½   small red onion

½   red bell pepper, seeded

3   cups coarsely chopped heirloom tomatoes, any variety

3   cups chopped peaches, pitted, not peeled

1   jalapeño, seeded

½   cup chopped fresh basil

1   tablespoon fresh tarragon leaves

1   dozen ice cubes

2   tablespoons extra virgin olive oil

1   tablespoon red wine vinegar

1   tablespoon lime juice

Sea salt and freshly ground black pepper

To prepare ingredients, chop onion, pepper, tomatoes and peaches into large chunks. With food processor running, drop in jalapeño, and process until minced. Turn off processor and scrape down sides. Add onion and process on pulse to coarsely chop. Repeat this procedure with the bell pepper, then the tomatoes, and finally with the peaches.

Transfer all ingredients to a medium pot or large bowl. Place basil and tarragon in food processor, pulse to chop and transfer to pot with tomato mixture. Place ice cubes in food processor, process into coarsely shaved ice chips and stir into soup. Stir in olive oil, red wine vinegar, lime juice and salt and pepper to taste. Cover and let sit 15 minutes to allow flavors to develop, but do not refrigerate. Stir again before serving.

SERVES 4

TIPS
Refrigeration changes the taste and texture of tomatoes, but the shaved ice in this recipe chills the soup and allows the tomatoes to maintain their integrity. If your fruit is particularly juicy, use less ice, and vice versa.

VARIATION
For a sweeter soup, substitute strawberries for a portion of either the tomatoes or peaches.

Golden Beet Soup

NOTHING SCREAMS CHILDHOOD MORE than the memory of the bottle of borscht my father kept stowed in the back of the refrigerator. I never dared to try it, and for years I avoided beets as a result. When I discovered fresh beets at the farm in a variety of beautiful colors, it took me a while to get up the nerve to bring them home and experiment. The leap to beet soup was even bigger, but the results were delicious.

2	pounds golden beets (about 5 medium beets)
1	medium yellow onion, chopped
1	tablespoon extra virgin olive oil, plus more for drizzling
2	teaspoons grated fresh ginger
1	tablespoon lemon juice
1	small baking potato
4	cups water
1	small red beet

Place golden beets in pot and cover with water. Bring to boil, cover and cook 45–60 minutes or until beets are tender and can be easily pierced with knife. Remove from heat and drain cooking water. Hold each beet under cold water and using your thumbs, peel by pushing away skin and root end. Chop beets into equal-size chunks and set aside.

In medium pot or Dutch oven over medium heat, sauté onion in olive oil until soft (about 3 minutes). Add ginger, lemon juice and golden beets. Peel and chop potato and add to pot. Pour in water and bring to boil. Reduce heat, cover and simmer 20 minutes or until potato is soft. Remove soup from heat and purée with handheld blender until smooth.

When ready to serve, hold red beet under cold running water and peel. Place silicone sheet over cutting board and finely grate beet over sheet. Serve soup topped with a pinch of grated red beet and a drizzle of olive oil.

SERVES 6

VARIATIONS
Instead of the red beet garnish, serve soup topped with crumbled goat cheese and a sprinkle of chopped chives. This soup can also be served cold.

Summer Squash with Lemon Cilantro Pesto

I'M ALWAYS EXCITED TO SEE THE BRIGHT ORANGE squash blossoms come out in my garden, but weeks later, when the zucchini and summer squash have taken over, I get desperate for new and different ways to prepare the same old staples. This dish looks like spaghetti with pesto, but tastes like so much more.

PESTO

1½	cups fresh cilantro
1	garlic clove, peeled
3	tablespoons plus 1 teaspoon pine nuts, toasted
1½	tablespoons lemon juice
3	tablespoons extra virgin olive oil
1	teaspoon lemon zest
¼	teaspoon sea salt

SQUASH

2	medium zucchini (about 8 inches each)
1	medium yellow summer squash (about 8 inches)

PREPARING PESTO

Place all ingredients except 1 teaspoon of pine nuts in food processor and purée until combined. Transfer to a medium bowl and set aside to allow flavors to blend.

PREPARING SQUASH

Slice zucchini and summer squash in half lengthwise and scoop out and discard seeds. Julienne the remaining squash. Place a steamer rack into a medium-size pot, add enough water to cover bottom of pot by 1 inch and bring to boil. Place all squash on steamer, cover and cook 3 minutes or until squash is just tender. Remove from heat, transfer squash to bowl with pesto and toss to combine. Top with remaining teaspoon of toasted pine nuts and serve.

SERVES 4

Warm Beet Salad with Red Onion, Mint and Pistachios

I ADORE EXPLORING FARMERS MARKETS, discovering seasonal produce and learning how the farmers are preparing their fresh produce. When I return, I wash and roast my beets immediately to keep them from disappearing in the bottom of my produce drawer and so that they'll be ready to add to salads with no additional preparation. There's just one catch. Once they're cooked, they're awfully hard to resist, and saving them for your recipe can be a challenge!

2	medium Chioggia beets with greens
1	medium golden beet with greens
1	medium red beet with greens
2	teaspoons sherry vinegar
1	small red onion, peeled
1	cup water
2	tablespoons chopped fresh mint
1	tablespoon extra virgin olive oil
	Sea salt and freshly ground black pepper
¼	cup coarsely chopped toasted pistachios

Preheat oven to 350°F.

Cut off beet stems and greens and set aside. Wash beets well and place in baking dish. Fill with enough water to just cover bottom, cover dish with foil and bake approximately 1 hour or until beets can be easily pierced with a knife (time will vary depending on size of beets). Remove from oven, uncover and set aside 5–6 minutes or until cool enough to touch. Peel and discard skin and cut beets into wedges or slices. Place Chioggia and golden beets in one bowl and red beets in another. Drizzle ¼ teaspoon sherry vinegar over red beets and ¾ teaspoon sherry vinegar over Chioggia and golden beets, toss to coat and set aside.

Wash and chop beet greens and place in colander. Slice onion into thin rounds and place over greens in colander. Bring water to boil and pour over greens and onion. Drain well and pat dry. Transfer to bowl and add mint and beets. Drizzle with remaining teaspoon sherry vinegar and olive oil. Season to taste with sea salt and pepper. Toss to evenly coat, top with chopped pistachios and serve.

SERVES 4

Cucumber Mint Salad

IN MY GARDEN, WE GROW PICKLING CUCUMBERS that are crisp, firm, slightly sweet and particularly easy to grow. Nevertheless, there are a variety of cucumbers that are much sweeter, juicier and, frankly, tastier than mine. This recipe will work with whatever cucumbers you have, but if you find yourself at a farmers market confronted with Sikkim, Poona Kheera or Lemon Cucumbers, you're in for a great treat, so don't be scared away by their nontraditional appearance.

---

3 medium cucumbers, any variety

¼ cup finely chopped red onion

1 teaspoon chopped fresh dill

¼ cup fresh mint leaves, torn

Coarse sea salt

DRESSING

2 tablespoons extra virgin olive oil

½ teaspoon maple syrup

1 teaspoon lime juice

Cut cucumbers into bite-size pieces. Place in bowl with onion, dill and mint. In separate bowl, whisk together all dressing ingredients. Drizzle evenly over cucumbers, season to taste with salt, and serve.

SERVES 4

TIP
If you don't care for cucumber seeds, you can scoop out and discard them before adding cucumbers to salad.

Daikon Carrot Salad with Cilantro and Peanuts

THIS SUMMER SLAW IS PARTICULARLY CLEANSING and refreshing and goes great with a piece of fish grilled simply, or alongside Seared Lemon Pepper Tofu *(page 80)*. For children, a meal-on-the-go or a fun appetizer, wrap this slaw into a summer roll.

---

2   cups julienned daikon

2   cups julienned carrots

2   cups thinly sliced
     Napa cabbage

1   jalapeño, seeded and
     julienned

½   cup chopped fresh cilantro

¾   cup dry roasted peanuts

DRESSING

1   tablespoon
     apple cider vinegar

1   tablespoon
     toasted sesame oil

1   tablespoon grapeseed oil

2   teaspoons
     brown rice syrup

1   teaspoon
     ume plum vinegar

1   teaspoon lime juice

¼   teaspoon sea salt

Place daikon, carrots, Napa cabbage, jalapeño and cilantro in large mixing bowl and toss to combine. In separate small bowl, whisk together all dressing ingredients. Drizzle dressing over salad and toss to evenly coat. Fold in roasted peanuts, and serve.

SERVES 4

Grilled Pattypan and Peaches with Green Chile Sauce

I'VE SPENT MOST OF MY LIFE shying away from hot peppers, until a recent trip to Santa Fe, where chile sauce was served on everything – breakfast, lunch and dinner. In short order, I was addicted and therefore highly motivated to figure out my own rendition of a green chile sauce to keep my cravings at bay. This sauce freezes well. I like to make extra to have it on hand so I don't have to start from scratch every time.

SAUCE

- 1 pound green chiles (Anaheim, cubanelle, poblano…)
- 1 garlic clove, peeled
- 2 tablespoons extra virgin olive oil

Sea salt

INDREDIENTS

- 1 large sweet onion, sliced into ½-inch rounds
- 3 pattypan squash, cut into ⅓-inch rounds
- 4 peaches, halved, pitted and cut into ½-inch slices

Extra virgin olive oil

Sea salt and freshly ground black pepper

PREPARING SAUCE

To roast chiles, either preheat oven to 450°F and roast chiles for 20 minutes or place them over gas grill or range until all sides are charred (about 10 minutes). Remove roasted chiles from heat and immediately place in sealable bowl or brown paper bag. Close bowl or bag and set aside for 10 minutes. Open, remove chiles, hold under running water, and peel off and discard skins. Pat chiles dry, slice open, and remove and discard stems and seeds. (Keep some seeds if you want to amp up the heat in your sauce.) With food processor running, drop in garlic and process until minced. Turn off processor, add chiles and olive oil and process until smooth. Add salt to taste and set aside to allow flavors to develop.

GRILLING

Preheat grill to medium.

Brush onion, pattypan squash and peaches with olive oil and sprinkle with salt and pepper. Place on grill and cook 4–5 minutes per side or until soft and cooked through. Remove from grill and serve topped with chile sauce.

SERVES 4

Polenta with Portobello Mushrooms, Greens and Tomato Vinaigrette

FRESHLY MADE CREAMY POLENTA IS EASY and satisfying and is the perfect canvas for a variety of roasted summer vegetables. I serve this recipe differently every time — it just depends on what looks best at the farmers market. Some of my favorite additions include Japanese eggplant, fennel and zucchini. For added decadence, top with crumbled goat cheese and pitted kalamata olives.

TOMATO VINAIGRETTE

1	garlic clove, chopped
½	cup extra virgin olive oil
1	tablespoon plus 1 teaspoon balsamic vinegar
½	cup packed combined herbs (parsley, sage and tarragon)
½	cup chopped fresh tomato (skins, seeds and all)

Sea salt and freshly ground black pepper

POLENTA

4	cups vegetable stock
1	cup polenta
¼	teaspoon sea salt

Freshly ground black pepper

VEGETABLES

2	red bell peppers
4	portobello mushrooms
1	medium sweet onion
2	cups packed arugula, baby spinach or mesclun mix

PREPARING VINAIGRETTE

Place garlic, olive oil, balsamic vinegar and herbs in mixing bowl and process with handheld blender to mince garlic and combine ingredients. Add tomato and process. Season with salt and pepper and set aside.

PREPARING POLENTA

Bring stock to boil and whisk in polenta. Reduce heat to medium and whisk for 15 minutes or until polenta is thick. Season with salt and pepper, cover and remove from heat until ready to serve.

PREPARING VEGETABLES

Preheat oven to 400°F and line baking sheet with parchment paper. Stem and seed bell peppers and cut into thick slices. Place on baking sheet and roast for 20 minutes. Remove from oven and transfer to bowl. Seal bowl and set aside.

Wipe mushroom caps, remove stems, and place underside facing up on baking sheet. Slice onion widthwise into ¼-inch slices and add to baking sheet. Place in oven and roast 20–25 minutes or until vegetables are soft (will depend on size). Remove from oven and set aside.

While vegetables roast, open bowl with peppers and peel away skins. If difficult to remove, hold and peel under running water.

To serve, scoop polenta into center of each dish, top with a handful of leafy greens, then portobello mushrooms, then pepper slices and then onion. Serve with vinaigrette drizzled over top or on the side.

SERVES 4

Chopped Salad with Blackberry Shallot Vinaigrette

CHOPPED SALADS ADD A SPLASH OF COLOR TO A MEAL. This one in particular is sure to wake up your palate with its varied tastes and textures, all complemented by the sweet blackberry vinaigrette. If you're making this salad in advance, keep the salad and dressing separate and hold off adding the tomatoes and avocado until just before serving.

1½ cups chopped fresh tomatoes

1 cup chopped green beans

1 orange bell pepper, chopped

¼ cup chopped radishes

½ head radicchio, chopped

2 avocados, pitted, peeled and chopped

2 tablespoons lemon juice

¼ cup toasted pine nuts

10 blackberries, halved

DRESSING

10 whole blackberries

1 shallot, minced

⅓ cup extra virgin olive oil

2 tablespoons red wine vinegar

1 tablespoon maple syrup

1 tablespoon lime juice

Sea salt and freshly ground black pepper

In large bowl, combine chopped tomatoes, green beans, bell pepper, radishes and radicchio. In separate small bowl, toss avocados with lemon juice to coat and then fold into salad.

Set fine-mesh strainer over a bowl, and place whole berries for dressing in strainer. Using the back of a wooden spoon, mash berries through strainer to separate juice from pulp and seeds. In small mixing bowl, whisk together 2 tablespoons of blackberry juice, shallot, olive oil, red wine vinegar, maple syrup, lime juice and salt and pepper to taste. Drizzle desired amount over salad. You may not need to use the entire amount of dressing. Top with pine nuts and halved blackberries, and serve.

SERVES 4

VARIATIONS
For a lighter dressing, substitute strawberries for the blackberries and omit the lime juice. In winter, substitute dried cranberries for the blackberries — simply soak in hot water to reconstitute, drain well, add to dressing, and purée all dressing ingredients with handheld blender.

Edamame Succotash

I CANNOT TAKE CREDIT FOR THIS RECIPE. It is from the kitchen of my publisher, who loves sharing his creations. From the moment this recipe hit my inbox, I was suspect. How could these traditional American tastes work when seasoned with Asian-style condiments? Please don't let him know that I've admitted this, but he was right, and I was wrong. I tweaked it slightly, but this one is indeed an ML original.

2 cups water

1 pound shelled edamame beans (about 1½ cups)

Sea salt

2 ears corn, cooked, kernels cut off (about 1½ cups kernels)

1½ cups cooked aduki beans

1 small red onion, diced

1 small orange bell pepper, diced

1 small red bell pepper, diced

1 tablespoon tamari

1 tablespoon toasted sesame oil

2 tablespoons toasted sesame seeds

In medium pot over high heat, bring water to boil. Add edamame beans and a few pinches of salt and cook uncovered for 3 minutes. Remove from heat, drain water and return edamame to pot. Add corn, beans, onion and bell peppers and toss to combine. Add tamari, sesame oil and sesame seeds, and fold to distribute all ingredients evenly. Serve warm or cold.

SERVES 4

Sesame Scallion Brown Rice Salad

I COULD PASS ON SWEETS MOST DAYS, but the combination of sweet, salty, bitter and sour in this dish is super-satisfying and right up my alley! Serve it warm or cold with Asian greens like pac choy or tatsoi, some marinated tofu or tempeh, a big green salad or just about anything off the grill.

---

1   cup short grain brown rice

2   cups water

Thumb-size piece kombu

1   orange bell pepper, chopped

1   mango, peeled, pitted and chopped

8   scallions, chopped

2   tablespoons chopped pickled sushi ginger

2   tablespoons toasted black sesame seeds

2   tablespoons toasted sesame oil

1½   teaspoons ume plum vinegar

Rinse rice and place in pot with water and kombu. Bring to boil, reduce heat, cover and simmer until liquid is absorbed. Remove from heat and set aside to cool before fluffing.

In separate bowl, combine bell pepper, mango, scallions, pickled ginger and sesame seeds. Remove kombu from rice and discard it. Fluff rice and add to bowl with vegetables. Drizzle with toasted sesame oil and ume plum vinegar, toss and serve.

SERVES 4

Fingerling Potatoes with Red Onion and Sage

MULTICOLORED FINGERLING POTATOES ARE PLENTIFUL at farmers markets in late summer. I am the annoying customer who digs through the basket looking for the smallest potatoes, for no reason other than I find them irresistibly cute. In truth, they all taste the same, so just grab a few handfuls and you'll be good to go. In the cold-weather months, enjoy this recipe by substituting baby red Bliss potatoes.

---

2   pounds fingerling potatoes

2   tablespoons
extra virgin olive oil

4   garlic cloves, minced

1   small red onion, chopped

1   bunch fresh sage
(about ¼ cup minced)

Coarse sea salt

Preheat oven to 375°F.

Wash potatoes and place in casserole. Drizzle with 1 tablespoon olive oil and roast for 35 minutes or until soft (time will depend on size of potatoes).

In a medium skillet over medium heat, sauté garlic and onion in remaining tablespoon olive oil until soft (about 3 minutes). Add sage and sauté 2 minutes longer. Remove from heat and set aside.

When soft, remove potatoes from oven and toss with onion-herb mixture. Season to taste with salt and serve.

SERVES 6

Green and Yellow Beans with Garlic and Herbs

LIGHT AND EASY IS MY SUMMER COOKING MOTTO. I much prefer enjoying myself outside as opposed to working in the kitchen, and lighter preparations let the fresh tastes of summer speak for themselves. This recipe comes straight from my garden, where the beans grow up the fence posts and I'm able to pick a handful of fresh herbs just outside my back door.

½ pound green beans, trimmed

½ pound yellow beans, trimmed

1 garlic clove, minced

2 tablespoons extra virgin olive oil

1 tablespoon fresh thyme leaves, minced

1 tablespoon lemon juice

1 tablespoon chopped fresh chives

Zest from ½ lemon

Coarse sea salt and freshly ground black pepper

Steam green and yellow beans until just tender and bright in color (about 4 minutes). Remove from heat, drain and set aside.

In small skillet over medium-low heat, sauté garlic in olive oil until soft (about 3 minutes). Add thyme and lemon juice and sauté 1 minute longer. Remove from heat, pour over beans and toss. Add chives, lemon zest, and salt and pepper to taste and serve.

SERVES 4

VARIATIONS
Lemon thyme or lemon balm can be substituted for the thyme. You can also turn up the heat in this recipe with a pinch of crushed red pepper flakes. I'm always surprised how welcome a little spice can be on a hot day!

Veggie Kebabs with Smokey Barbeque Sauce

THERE'S SOMETHING ABOUT SUMMER GRILLING that immediately brings ribs to mind, at least for my husband, who didn't know what a vegan was until he married one. This barbeque sauce definitely satisfies his sense of longing, and is great for grilling just about anything. It requires a little advance preparation, so be sure to plan ahead.

SAUCE
1   small red onion, chopped

3   garlic cloves, chopped

2   tablespoons extra virgin olive oil

4   cups chopped tomatoes

½   cup maple syrup

¼   cup molasses

½   cup apple cider vinegar

2   teaspoons mustard powder

1   teaspoon chile powder

1   teaspoon sea salt

1   teaspoon freshly ground black pepper

Paprika to taste

KEBABS
12   cremini mushrooms, stems removed

1   orange bell pepper, cut into squares

8   cherry tomatoes

1   small zucchini, cut into chunks

1   small yellow summer squash, cut into chunks

PREPARING SAUCE
In Dutch oven over medium heat, sauté onion and garlic in olive oil until soft. Add remaining ingredients and stir to combine. Bring to boil, reduce to simmer and cook uncovered for 1 hour. Purée with handheld blender and cook 30 minutes longer or until thick. Remove from heat and set aside to bring to room temperature. Transfer to sealable glass containers and refrigerate or freeze until ready to use.

MAKING KEBABS
If using wooden skewers, soak in water for 15 minutes before making kebabs. Preheat grill to medium.

Assemble kebabs by skewering vegetables in alternating pattern. Brush with barbeque sauce and place side by side on grill. Grill each side for 3 minutes, brush tops with more sauce and flip. Repeat until vegetables are cooked through and each side is lightly seared. Remove from grill and serve.

SERVES 4

TIP
This recipe yields approximately 4½ cups of barbeque sauce – plenty for your kebabs and more!

Tempeh with Apricots and Capers

TEMPEH IS A GREAT SOURCE OF PROTEIN that's light enough for a snack and satisfying enough as a main dish, too. Tempeh comes in many varieties that feature a variety of ingredients. I like the garden style with vegetables for this recipe, but experiment to find the one you like best. For an extra hit of protein and energy, top with toasted pumpkin seeds or pistachios.

8	ounces tempeh
2	garlic cloves, minced
½	small red onion, minced (about ¼ cup)
3	tablespoons extra virgin olive oil
1	cup pitted and chopped apricots
½	small fennel bulb, cored and chopped (about 1 cup)
¼	cup capers
1	tablespoon mirin
2	tablespoons lemon juice
2	tablespoons apricot juice
¼	cup chopped fresh basil
	Sea salt and freshly ground black pepper

Cut tempeh into large pieces and steam for 5 minutes. Remove from heat and set aside to cool slightly.

In large skillet over medium heat, sauté garlic and onion in 1 tablespoon olive oil. Add apricots, fennel and capers and stir. Add mirin and sauté 2 minutes longer or until apricots are lightly seared. Coarsely chop or crumble tempeh and add to skillet.

In small bowl, combine lemon juice, apricot juice, basil and remaining 2 tablespoons olive oil. Add to tempeh mixture and sauté to combine flavors and heat through. Remove from heat, season to taste with salt and pepper and serve warm or chilled.

SERVES 4

SERVING SUGGESTION
Accompany this dish with lightly steamed asparagus, wedges of cantaloupe or a steamed artichoke.

VARIATION
Carry this recipe into your fall menus by substituting dried apricots for the fresh.

Seared Lemon Pepper Tofu

BY THE TIME I STARTED TO LEARN HOW TO COOK, I was primarily interested in vegan fare. Then one day a friend asked me to prepare chicken cutlets as part of a meal, so I called my mother for help. I'll never forget her response. "Anything you can do with tofu, you can do with chicken!" In the end, my friends were thrilled with the Lemon Pepper Chicken, and I've been making it with tofu ever since. I hope you enjoy it, too.

---

1 pound fresh tofu, cut into ½-inch fillets

2 garlic cloves, minced

2 tablespoons extra virgin olive oil

4 tablespoons lemon juice

2 tablespoons mirin

Freshly ground black pepper

Zest of 1 lemon

¼ teaspoon crushed red pepper flakes

Wrap tofu in towel and gently press out excess liquid.

Heat large cast-iron skillet to medium and sauté garlic in olive oil for 2 minutes. Add 1 tablespoon lemon juice, 1 tablespoon mirin and plenty of pepper. Stir to combine and place tofu in pan. Sauté 4 minutes, flip fillets, add another 1 tablespoon lemon juice and more pepper as desired. Sauté 4 minutes longer, flip tofu again, add 1 tablespoon lemon juice and final tablespoon mirin. Sauté 4 minutes or until evenly browned. Flip one last time, add remaining 1 tablespoon lemon juice, lemon zest and crushed red pepper and sauté 4 minutes or until evenly browned. Remove from heat and serve.

SERVES 2

TIP
Steaming tofu before searing it allows it to absorb more flavor and has the added benefit of making it easier to digest.

Penne and Roasted Vegetables with Basil Sauce

I COULD PRACTICALLY SURVIVE ON HEIRLOOM TOMATOES and basil all summer long – which is a good thing, as once the garden starts producing, there is rarely a night that we're without! Roasting is a great alternative to the everyday tomato, cucumber and basil platter with olive oil and sea salt. Not only does roasting bring out the sweetness of the tomatoes, but it opens the door for other presentations and combinations, like this one.

½ pound penne-style pasta of choice

1 fennel bulb, halved, cored and sliced into thin strips

1 orange bell pepper, cut into strips

3 tablespoons extra virgin olive oil, plus more for drizzling

3 garlic cloves, not peeled

4–5 medium tomatoes, cut into chunks

½ cup firmly packed fresh basil leaves

¼ teaspoon sea salt

Coarse sea salt and freshly ground black pepper

2 tablespoons chopped fresh flat-leaf parsley

Preheat oven to 400°F.

Cook pasta according to directions on package. Drain, rinse and leave in colander until ready to serve.

Meanwhile, combine fennel and bell pepper in glass roasting dish and drizzle with enough olive oil to coat lightly. Wrap garlic cloves in foil and place both garlic and vegetables in oven to roast for 12 minutes. Remove vegetables from oven, add tomatoes and return to oven to roast for an additional 8 minutes or until tomatoes are warm throughout and just soft. Remove vegetables and garlic from oven and set aside.

Place basil in small bowl and cover with boiling water. Let sit 15 seconds, then drain and press to remove any excess water. Transfer basil to blender or food processor. Peel and discard skins from garlic cloves and add to basil. Add olive oil and salt and process to desired consistency.

Transfer pasta to serving dish. Using a slotted spoon, add roasted vegetables and toss. Add enough juice from roasting to just moisten pasta. Add basil sauce and salt and pepper to taste, and toss to combine. Top with chopped parsley and serve.

SERVES 4

Energy Squares

THESE SQUARES ARE AS POPULAR WITH THE ADULTS in my family as they are with the children, whether we're headed out for a hike, a run, a bike ride or even a road trip. Of course, they also make a delicious and satisfying year-round snack. Add your favorite toasted nuts, seeds or even dried fruit to suit your tastes and make your own unique creation.

1	cup peanut butter (almond, cashew and sunflower butters can be substituted)
⅓	cup brown rice syrup
⅓	cup maple syrup
1¼	cups crispy brown rice cereal
½	cup toasted almonds
½	cup unsweetened shredded coconut
¾	cup ground flax seeds
¼	cup gluten- and dairy-free chocolate chips

In medium pot over low heat, whisk together peanut butter, brown rice syrup and maple syrup. Remove from heat and set aside.

In separate bowl, combine rice cereal, almonds, coconut and ground flax. Fold dry ingredients into peanut butter mixture until all ingredients are incorporated.

Rinse 8 x 8-inch baking dish with cold water to prevent sticking. Spoon in batter, sprinkle with chocolate chips and press firmly and evenly into dish. Refrigerate for 45 minutes or until firm. Remove from refrigerator, cut into squares and store in airtight container.

MAKES approximately 36 bite-size squares

Grilled Peaches with Raspberry Syrup and Toasted Almonds

AS SIMPLY SWEET AS THIS DESSERT IS, it somehow feels quite decadent as well. Grill the peaches while making the rest of your dinner so they're ready to go for dessert. Then all you have to do is make the sauce and you're set. Of course, a scoop of vanilla rice cream or ice cream is always a welcome finish.

6	peaches, halved and pitted
12	ounces raspberries, fresh or frozen
3	tablespoons maple syrup
¾	teaspoon arrowroot powder
½	cup toasted slivered almonds

Preheat grill to medium.

Leaving skins on, cut peaches into quarters or leave in halves, as desired. Place peaches flesh-side down on grill and cook 4–6 minutes or until just starting to bubble. Time will vary according to size and ripeness of peaches. Flip peaches and grill on skin side for another 6–8 minutes or until very soft. Remove from grill and set aside.

Place 8 ounces of raspberries and all the maple syrup in small pot over medium heat. Cook, stirring, until berries break down. Remove from heat and pour syrup through a fine-mesh strainer into a separate bowl to remove seeds. Return syrup to pot and whisk in arrowroot. Continue whisking until syrup starts to thicken. Remove from heat, place peaches in individual serving dishes as desired, and drizzle each serving with syrup. Top with fresh berries and a sprinkle of toasted almonds and serve.

SERVES 6

Black Currant Plum Crisp

CRISPS ARE SO EASY TO MAKE and so satisfying – whether you're serving them for breakfast, a snack or dessert. Make sure your plums are ripe, and be sure to select a variety of plum that is more sweet than tart to avoid ending up with an overly tart crisp. A scoop of vanilla rice cream or ice cream is the perfect accompaniment.

FILLING

2½	pounds plums (10–12)
½	cup dried currants
2–3	dashes ground nutmeg
	Pinch of sea salt
¼	cup maple syrup
¼	cup ivory teff flour

CRISP

1	cup almond meal
1	cup ivory teff flour
¼	cup sliced almonds
	Pinch of ground nutmeg
	Pinch of sea salt
¼	cup virgin coconut oil
¼	cup maple syrup
½	teaspoon vanilla extract

Preheat oven to 350°F.

PREPARING FILLING

Leaving skins on, halve plums, remove and discard pits and slice into thin wedges (about ¼ inch thick). Place in large mixing bowl and set aside.

In small pot over medium heat, place currants with just enough water to cover, bring to boil and simmer 5 minutes to soften and plump. Drain well and add to bowl with plums. Add nutmeg and salt, and stir. Add maple syrup and teff flour and stir until plums are evenly coated and ingredients are combined. Pour mixture into 8 x 8-inch casserole and set aside.

PREPARING CRISP

Using same mixing bowl, combine almond meal, teff flour, almonds, nutmeg and salt. Over low heat, melt coconut oil in small skillet. Remove from heat, whisk in maple syrup and vanilla and pour over flour mixture. Stir to combine and crumble over plum mixture.

Bake 45 minutes or until top is golden brown and plums are soft. Remove from oven, and cool slightly before serving.

SERVES 6

Blueberry Tart

"EAT MORE THAN YOU BRING HOME" is our family rule of thumb for blueberry picking. By the time we're done, we're often left with tummy aches all-around, and not enough blueberries to make more than a few muffins or pancakes. All I have to do is mention this tart before we start picking and our blueberry yield miraculously increases — and our tummy aches magically disappear!

CRUST

2   cups almond meal

2   tablespoons maple syrup

1   tablespoon virgin coconut oil

Pinch of sea salt

1   teaspoon almond extract

FILLING

1   cup apple juice

2   tablespoons arrowroot powder

½   cup maple syrup

2   tablespoons lemon juice

¼   teaspoon almond extract

Zest of 1 lemon

Pinch of sea salt

2   cups blueberries

Preheat oven to 350°F. Lightly oil 9-inch tart pan.

PREPARING CRUST

Place almond meal in large mixing bowl. In small skillet over medium-low heat, whisk together maple syrup, coconut oil and salt until oil melts. Whisk in almond extract and remove from heat. Pour this mixture over the almond meal and fold to incorporate all ingredients. Transfer dough to tart pan and press to form crust. Bake 15 minutes or until golden brown. Remove from oven and, using the back of a wooden spoon, gently press down any puffed areas of crust. Set crust on wire rack to cool.

PREPARING FILLING

In small bowl, whisk together ½ cup apple juice with arrowroot and set aside. In medium Dutch oven over medium heat, combine remaining ½ cup apple juice with maple syrup, lemon juice, almond extract, lemon zest and salt and bring to simmer. Add 1 cup blueberries and stir until berries start to pop and liquid turns red/blue. Reduce heat to low and whisking continuously, pour arrowroot-juice mixture into berry mixture. When liquid is thick, remove from heat and fold in remaining blueberries. Pour into crust, spread evenly and refrigerate for at least 1 hour to set.

SERVES 8

FALL

Carrot Cashew Miso Spread

EVERY WEEKEND AT THE FARM, my friend Kathy sells her incredible sourdough breads and they are impossible to resist. I created this recipe especially to go with her delicious rustica bread…after all, a girl can eat only so many loaves of bread dipped in extra virgin olive oil! As it turns out, I like this spread every bit as much on crackers, on a piece of toasted rice bread, or in a tofu and sprout sandwich.

2   large carrots
¾   cup raw cashews
1   cup vegetable stock
2   tablespoons light miso
Toasted ivory and/or
    black sesame seeds

Peel carrots and discard dry ends. Chop into ½-inch pieces and place in pot with cashews and stock. Turn heat to high and bring to boil. Reduce heat to medium and cook until carrots are cooked through (about 10 minutes).

Remove from heat and, using slotted spoon, scoop carrots and cashews into food processor. In separate bowl, measure out ¼ cup of cooking liquid and dissolve miso in it. Add to bowl with carrots and process until smooth. Serve topped with sesame seeds, or refrigerate in airtight container for up to 4 days.

MAKES about 1½ cups

Green Fries

I LOVE FRESHLY BAKED BREAD, but try hard to resist it when I'm out to eat. What I really want is something to bridge the gap until my meal arrives and not fill me up so that I don't have room for dessert! My local burger joint has the perfect solution – hot, salty, crunchy and healthy "green fries." Somehow, when I tried making them myself, the addition of wasabi powder became a must.

1	pound green beans
¼	cup grapeseed oil
¼	teaspoon coarse sea salt
¼	teaspoon wasabi powder

Trim green beans, discard dry ends and/or stems and pat dry (this will reduce splattering oil when you fry them). Line plate with paper towel and set on counter next to burner.

Place oil in medium Dutch oven over high heat. When oil is hot, use tongs to place a small batch of beans in pot and quickly cover to avoid splattering oil. Give pot a shake every 10 seconds to ensure even cooking and fry a total of 30 seconds until beans are bright green and just soft. Remove from pot and place on paper towel. Repeat until all beans are cooked and pat with a paper towel to absorb excess oil.

In separate bowl, combine salt and wasabi powder. Sprinkle over beans, toss to evenly coat and serve.

SERVES 4

VARIATIONS
Combine salt with other spices as desired. Some of my favorites are mustard powder, cumin, curry and even lemon zest. Combine with salt, sprinkle on veggies, toss and serve. In spring, this recipe is irresistible with asparagus spears. Carrot sticks are delicious too, but you'll have to change the name of the recipe!

Red Lentil Soup with Turnip and Parsley

WHEN THAT FIRST COLD RAINY FALL DAY ROLLS AROUND and you find yourself yearning to put a pot of soup on the stove, this soup is the answer. It's the perfect use for the final baskets of tomatoes from your garden or the farmers market, and a great way to feature fall's bounty of sweet turnips.

1½ cups dried red lentils

3 cups water

Thumb-size piece kombu

1 medium yellow onion, diced

4 garlic cloves, minced

3 celery stalks, diced

2 tablespoons extra virgin olive oil

2 tablespoons mirin

1½ cups chopped tomatoes

1 turnip, peeled and diced

1½ cups cooked great northern beans

4 cups vegetable stock

Sea salt and freshly ground black pepper

½ cup fresh flat-leaf parsley

Rinse and drain lentils. Place in pot with water and kombu and bring to boil. Skim and discard foam. Reduce heat to simmer, partially cover and cook until lentils are soft (about 20 minutes). Remove from heat and set aside.

In soup pot or Dutch oven over medium heat, sauté onion, garlic and celery in oil until soft (4–6 minutes). Add mirin, tomatoes, turnip and beans. Stir to combine ingredients. Remove and discard kombu from lentils and add lentils to soup pot. Add stock, bring to boil, reduce heat and simmer covered for 20 minutes. Season to taste with salt and pepper and remove from heat. Stir in ⅓ cup chopped parsley and serve topped with remaining parsley as garnish.

SERVES 8

VARIATIONS
Hakurei turnips, the size of a dime, are super-sweet and a great variety for this soup. They often are sold with their greens on. If so, simply cut off the greens, halve the turnips, add as directed and then stir in the greens just before serving. Alternatively, you can substitute yellow split peas for the lentils.

Tomato Saffron Soup

TOMATO SOUP IS A TALL ORDER – not because of the level of difficulty or because we crave it in winter when tomatoes are not in season, but rather, because we can never compete with the memory of the "soup from a can" that we so enjoyed as kids. Best to stray just enough to avoid direct comparison! The saffron in this soup definitely will not let your taste buds down and will set an even higher bar for the next generation of tomato soup lovers.

---

1   large yellow onion, chopped

5   garlic cloves, peeled and minced

2   tablespoons extra virgin olive oil

3   stalks celery

½   fennel bulb

2   tablespoons mirin

Pinch of saffron threads, crumbled, or ⅛ teaspoon saffron powder

6   cups chopped tomatoes (fresh or canned; see tip)

1   bay leaf

2   tablespoons chopped fresh basil

2   tablespoons chopped fresh parsley

1   teaspoon maple syrup

2   cups vegetable stock

Sea salt and freshly ground black pepper

Zest of 1 orange

In soup pot or Dutch oven over medium heat, sauté onion and garlic in olive oil 3 minutes or until soft. Chop celery and fennel into ¼-inch pieces and add to pot. Continue sautéing 4 minutes or until vegetables are soft. Add mirin and saffron and stir. Add tomatoes, bay leaf, basil, parsley, maple syrup and vegetable stock. Stir to combine and simmer covered for 20 minutes. Remove from heat and purée with handheld blender. Season to taste with salt and pepper. Top each serving with a pinch of orange zest and serve.

SERVES 6

TIP

If using fresh tomatoes, score tops with an "x" and immerse them in boiling water for 15 seconds. Remove with slotted spoon and set aside until cool enough to touch. Then, gently peel away and discard skins. If tomatoes have many seeds, cut in half, scoop out and discard them.

Hearty Minestrone

I LIKE MY SOUP PACKED WITH GOODNESS and didn't name this recipe casually. Hearty is almost an understatement! It's incredibly easy to prepare and encourages lots of improvisation, so experiment freely with different legumes and leafy greens. This soup comes together quickly and has more depth of flavor on day two.

1	medium yellow onion, diced
3	stalks celery, diced
1	tablespoon extra virgin olive oil, plus more for dizzling
1½	cups cooked great northern beans
3	carrots, thinly sliced
3	cups chopped tomatoes
1½	cups cooked chickpeas
1½	cups cooked kidney beans
1	head broccoli with stems, cut into small pieces (about 1 cup)
1½	cups trimmed and chopped green beans
5	cups vegetable stock
1	tablespoon balsamic vinegar
1	bay leaf
3	tablespoons chopped fresh parsley
2	tablespoons chopped fresh basil
2	tablespoons chopped fresh oregano
½	teaspoon sea salt, or more to taste

Freshly ground black pepper

In soup pot or large Dutch oven over medium heat, sauté onion and celery in olive oil 4–6 minutes or until soft. Add great northern beans and using a potato masher, mash most of the beans (this will thicken base of soup slightly).

Add carrots, tomatoes, chickpeas, kidney beans, broccoli, green beans, vegetable stock, balsamic vinegar, bay leaf, parsley, basil, oregano, salt and plenty of pepper. Bring to boil, reduce heat, cover and simmer 30 minutes. Remove from heat, discard bay leaf and season to taste with extra salt. Serve topped with a drizzle of olive oil.

SERVES 8

SERVING SUGGESTION
Top with a squeeze of fresh lemon juice and/or stir in a tablespoon of Parsley Walnut Pesto *(page 100)* before serving.

Ginger Shiitake Soup with Cabbage and Edamame Beans

FRESH SHIITAKE MUSHROOMS ARE AVAILABLE YEAR-ROUND at my local farm. While I bring them home with the best of intentions, I've been known to forget about them until one day I open that brown bag and discover dried mushrooms. Fortunately, once dried they offer an even stronger taste that is just perfect for making a savory stock for soups like this one. Don't worry, you can buy them dried at most natural food or Asian grocery stores.

12	dried shiitake mushrooms
8	cups water
1	heaping tablespoon grated fresh ginger
1	large leek, chopped
1	tablespoon grapeseed oil
2	cups Napa or green cabbage, thinly sliced
1	carrot, shredded
1	cup edamame beans, shelled
2	tablespoons tamari
1	teaspoon ume plum vinegar
	Toasted or hot sesame oil

Place whole mushrooms in pot with water and bring to boil. Remove from heat, cover and let sit for 30 minutes (mushrooms will become very soft). With slotted spoon, remove mushrooms, discard stems and slice caps into thin strips. Set mushrooms and stock aside separately.

In soup pot or large Dutch oven over medium heat, sauté ginger and leek in oil until soft (about 3 minutes). Add shiitakes and sauté 4–5 minutes or until mushrooms start to brown. Add cabbage, carrots, edamame beans, tamari and water left over from soaking shiitakes. Cover and simmer 10 minutes or until carrots are soft. Remove from heat, stir in ume plum vinegar, top individual servings with toasted or hot sesame oil as desired and serve.

SERVES 6

VARIATIONS
For a more protein-rich soup, add cubed firm silken tofu. For a heartier meal, prepare 8 ounces of soba or udon noodles and divide among each serving.

Medley of Pestos

FEW THINGS TASTE LIKE SUMMER more than freshly made pesto. All fall long, I harvest my herbs and make pesto – hopefully enough to freeze and last through winter. Each pesto lends its unique flavor to enhance your recipes, whether you are tossing it with grilled vegetables, serving as a dip or spread, adding a dollop to soup or using as the base for marinade or aioli.

BASIC BASIL PESTO

2   garlic cloves, peeled
1   cup toasted pine nuts
2½   cups packed
     fresh basil leaves
½   cup extra virgin olive oil,
     plus more as needed
1   tablespoon lemon juice
Sea salt

With food processor running, drop in garlic and process until minced. Turn off processor, scrape down sides and add pine nuts, basil, olive oil and lemon juice. Process to mince all ingredients and combine. Season to taste with salt and thin with extra olive oil to achieve desired consistency. Refrigerate or freeze in airtight container until ready to use.

MAKES 1 cup

PARSLEY WALNUT PESTO

2   garlic cloves, peeled
1   cup toasted walnuts
1½   cups packed
     flat-leaf parsley leaves
¼   cup extra virgin olive oil,
     plus more as needed
2   tablespoons lemon juice
Sea salt

With food processor running, drop in garlic and process until minced. Turn off processor, scrape down sides and add walnuts, parsley, olive oil and lemon juice. Process to mince all ingredients and combine. Season to taste with salt and thin with extra olive oil to achieve desired consistency. Refrigerate or freeze in airtight container until ready to use.

MAKES ¾ cup

CILANTRO GINGER PEANUT PESTO

2   garlic cloves, peeled
2   teaspoons grated fresh ginger
½   cup dry roasted peanuts
1½   cups packed
     fresh cilantro leaves
¼   cup extra virgin olive oil,
     plus more as needed
2   tablespoons lime juice
Sea salt

With food processor running, drop in garlic and process until minced. Turn off processor, scrape down sides and add ginger, peanuts, cilantro, olive oil, lime juice and salt. Process to mince all ingredients and combine. Season to taste with extra salt and thin with extra olive oil to achieve desired consistency. Refrigerate or freeze in airtight container until ready to use.

MAKES ¾ cup

Green Beans, Figs and Pistachios in Balsamic Reduction

THE FLAVORS AND TEXTURES IN THIS DISH ARE BIG, so keep it simple as you plan the rest of your meal. I like to serve it with a piece of grilled fish or tofu – dressed simply with olive oil, salt and pepper. Add a wedge of cantaloupe for a beautiful contrast in color and taste.

---

6   fresh or dried figs
of choice

½   red onion,
cut into thin wedges

1   pound green beans
or haricots verts,
ends trimmed

3   tablespoons
vegetable stock

3   tablespoons balsamic
vinegar

Sea salt and freshly ground
black pepper

¾   cup shelled
roasted pistachios

If using fresh figs, carefully trim and discard tough stems, cut fruit lengthwise into quarters and set aside.

If using dried figs, trim and discard tops and steam figs 4 minutes. Add onion and green beans and steam 4 minutes longer or until beans are bright green and onions are soft. Remove from heat and transfer to mixing bowl.

In saucepan over medium heat, combine vegetable stock and balsamic vinegar. When mixture starts to bubble, reduce heat to medium-low, stir continuously and simmer until liquid reduces by half. Remove from heat, drizzle over bean mixture (if using fresh figs, add them now) and toss. Season to taste with salt and pepper and serve topped with pistachios.

SERVES 4

Pan-Seared Sweet Corn

I REALLY DON'T EVER GET TIRED OF CORN ON THE COB, but out of necessity, I started experimenting when my daughter had braces put on her teeth and we had to do away with the cobs. I owe her a thank-you, as this recipe was an instant hit. I love it as a side dish, but she likes it even more in a taco shell with chopped avocado and tomatoes. While the season for locally grown sweet corn is short where I live, we carry this recipe into early winter with fresh frozen sweet corn.

---

8   ears sweet corn
    (about 4 cups)

½   red onion, diced

3   garlic cloves, minced

1   tablespoon
    extra virgin olive oil

1   jalapeño, seeded and
    minced

½   red bell pepper, diced

2   pinches chile powder

2   pinches paprika

1   tablespoon lime juice

Sea salt and freshly ground
    black pepper

Chopped fresh parsley
    or cilantro

To prepare sweet corn, remove husks and silks and bring 2 inches water to boil in large pot. Add corn, cover and cook 5–6 minutes or until kernels are just tender. Remove from heat and set aside until cool enough to touch.

Alternatively, preheat grill to high. Pull back husks, remove corn silk and pull husks back over corn. Soak ears in cool water for 10 minutes and drain. Place on grill and cook for 15 minutes or until tender. Remove from heat and set aside until cool enough to touch.

In large skillet over medium heat, sauté onion and garlic in olive oil until soft (about 3 minutes). Add jalapeño and bell pepper and sauté 2 minutes longer. Slice corn from cob and add to skillet along with chile powder and paprika. Sauté on high for 2 minutes, stirring continuously, and sear kernels. Add lime juice and season to taste with salt and black pepper. Remove from heat, fold in parsley or cilantro and serve.

SERVES 4

Cabbage Sauté with Tart Cherries and Crisp Apples

WE ENJOY FRESHLY MADE COLESLAW all summer long. So by the time fall rolls around, this cooked sweet preparation comes as a welcome change. I like my cabbage wilted and just soft, but you may like yours cooked through. If so, simply sauté until you've reached your desired texture.

1	medium yellow onion, cut into thin wedges
1½	tablespoons grapeseed oil
3	cups thinly sliced red cabbage
3	cups thinly sliced green cabbage
1	cup dried unsweetened cherries
2	tablespoons mirin
1	Macoun apple (or tart, firm variety of choice)

Sea salt

DRESSING

2	tablespoons mustard seeds
2	tablespoons brown rice syrup
1½	teaspoons apple cider vinegar
2	tablespoons apple cider or juice

In Dutch oven over medium heat, sauté onion in oil 6 minutes or until very soft. Stir in cabbages, cherries and mirin and continue sautéing until cabbage starts to soften (about 4 minutes). Remove from heat and set aside.

In small dry skillet over low heat, lightly toast mustard seeds 2 minutes or until fragrant, being careful not to burn. Add brown rice syrup, apple cider vinegar and apple cider, and whisk 1 minute. Remove from heat and set aside.

Core apple and cut into ¼-inch matchsticks. Return cabbage to medium heat, add apple, drizzle with dressing and fold to coat evenly and heat through. Season to taste with salt, remove from heat and serve.

SERVES 4

TIP
If making this dish in advance, reheat it and add apples just before serving.

VARIATIONS
For a change, substitute caraway or fennel seeds for the mustard seeds.

Pan-Seared Tofu with Ginger Lime Glaze

MY MOTHER OFTEN HAS LEFTOVER SAUTÉED TOFU in her refrigerator and I simply can't keep from sneaking a taste (okay, so I usually finish it). I came up with this recipe so that I could enjoy leftovers whenever I wanted and without the drive to Mom's. My children (and their friends) devour this tofu before it ever reaches the table, but I like it even better a few hours later when it firms up.

---

1 pound fresh firm tofu (not silken), drained

2 tablespoons extra virgin olive oil

1 tablespoon grated fresh ginger

2 tablespoons tamari

2 tablespoons lime juice

2 tablespoons maple syrup

Slice tofu into fillets or cubes as desired. Heat sauté pan over medium heat. Add olive oil and ginger and sauté 1 minute. In small bowl, whisk together tamari, lime juice and maple syrup. Place tofu in skillet and add tamari mixture. Sauté tofu 3–4 minutes on each side. If pan gets dry, deglaze by adding 2 tablespoons water and continue sautéing until both sides of tofu are browned and firm. For a thicker glazed finish, deglaze pan with a second mixture of oil, ginger, tamari, lime juice and maple syrup. Remove from heat and serve.

SERVES 3

TIPS
A nonstick surface will prevent tofu from glazing. Use stainless steel or cast iron for best results. The more batches of tofu you sear, the more caramelized your glaze will become. This recipe doubles easily and you'll be grateful for the leftovers.

SERVING SUGGESTIONS
This tofu is a perfect addition to stir-fries, a hearty sandwich-stuffer and a delicious high-protein side dish or snack.

Basmati Rice with Leeks, Shiitakes and Arame

THIS BASIC RICE IS THE PERFECT COMPLEMENT to the bitter greens, sweet roots and hearty winter squashes that are the very essence of the fall harvest. Fresh or dried shiitake mushrooms work equally well in this recipe, and the arame adds an always-welcome dose of alkalinizing minerals.

1   cup brown basmati rice

Thumb-size piece kombu

2   cups water or vegetable stock

½   cup dried arame

3   cups water

15–20 shiitake mushrooms (dried or fresh)

1   large leek, thinly sliced

2   garlic cloves, minced

1   tablespoon extra virgin olive oil

Ume plum vinegar

Place rice in pot or rice cooker with kombu and 2 cups water or stock. Bring to boil, reduce to simmer and cook covered until liquid is absorbed (about 35 minutes). Remove from heat and set aside.

While rice is cooking, place arame in bowl, cover with 1 cup water and soak 15 minutes or until soft. Drain water, chop arame into small pieces and set aside.

If using dried mushrooms, bring 2 cups water to boil. Place mushrooms in bowl, cover with boiling water and soak until soft. Drain water, place mushrooms on towel and press out excess water. Trim and discard stems from mushrooms. Slice caps thinly and set aside.

In large sauté pan over medium heat, sauté leek and garlic in oil until soft. Add mushrooms, stir and continue sautéing 10 minutes or until mushrooms are brown, adding water 1 tablespoon at a time as needed to deglaze pan. Add arame and sauté to heat through (about 2 minutes). Remove from heat, fluff rice with fork or wooden spoon and fold in mushroom mixture. Season to taste with ume plum vinegar and serve.

SERVES 4

Sautéed Greens with Leeks and Garlic

THIS BASIC PREPARATION OF GREENS takes my family through all the seasons and is particularly delicious when we pick the greens from our garden. While the rest of my garden is put to bed for winter, kale and collard greens flourish in cold weather. I've even found myself trudging through the snow to pick them! Experiment with kale, collards, mustard greens, dandelion greens, chard or a combination of all.

3   garlic cloves, minced

1   large leek, sliced crosswise

1   tablespoon
    extra virgin olive oil

2   bunches assorted dark
    leafy greens, chopped

2   tablespoons mirin

Ume plum vinegar

Toasted sesame seeds

In large skillet or Dutch oven over medium heat, sauté garlic and leek in olive oil until soft (about 3 minutes). Add greens and mirin and sauté until greens are bright green and tender (about 4 minutes). Remove from heat, drizzle lightly with ume plum vinegar, sprinkle with sesame seeds and serve.

SERVES 4

VARIATIONS
Substitute 1 red onion or sweet onion for the leek, or add grated fresh ginger and/or turmeric.

Balsamic Glazed Roasted Root Vegetables

ROASTING IS ONE OF THE EASIEST WAYS to prepare root vegetables. I tend to make a large quantity (at least double this recipe) so that I can serve them at a second meal tossed with a whole grain or puréed with vegetable stock into a creamy soup. For a surprisingly different taste and a dish that's equally yummy, substitute apple cider vinegar for the balsamic.

2   rutabagas, peeled

6   parsnips, peeled

4   carrots, peeled

2   turnips, peeled

2   large leeks,
    sliced crosswise

2   tablespoons
    extra virgin olive oil

3   tablespoons
    balsamic vinegar

1   tablespoon chopped
    fresh rosemary
    (or 1 teaspoon dried)

Coarse sea salt

Preheat oven to 400°F.

Chop rutabagas, parsnips, carrots, turnips and leeks to uniform size. Place in large mixing bowl, drizzle with olive oil and balsamic vinegar, add rosemary and toss to combine. Pour vegetables into two 9 x 13-inch ovenproof casseroles and roast for 35 minutes or until soft. Roasting time will vary depending on how large or small vegetables are cut. Remove from heat, toss with salt to taste, and serve.

SERVES 4

VARIATIONS

Turn leftovers into soup by placing in soup pot or Dutch oven over high heat. Add enough stock to almost cover vegetables. Bring to boil, reduce heat and simmer until vegetables are heated through (about 5 minutes). Remove from heat and purée with handheld blender until smooth or desired consistency is reached. Adjust taste with any or all of the following: apple cider, orange juice, ground cinnamon, ground ginger, ground nutmeg, ground cloves, curry powder or ground cumin.

Spaghetti Squash with Capers, Tomatoes and Watercress

SPAGHETTI SQUASH SATISFIES EVERYONE IN MY FAMILY. It's fun like spaghetti, sweet like winter squash, and can be prepared simply by tossing it with tomato sauce, pesto or your favorite pasta accompaniment. This is one of my favorite combinations as the bitter greens and salty capers provide balance to the sweet squash and tomatoes.

1	spaghetti squash
½	yellow onion, diced
4	garlic cloves, minced
2	tablespoons extra virgin olive oil
2	tablespoons capers
1½	cups chopped tomatoes with their juices
2	tablespoons chopped fresh oregano
1	bunch watercress

Sea salt and freshly ground black pepper

Preheat oven to 400°F.

Halve squash, scoop out seeds and place facedown in roasting dish. Add enough water to cover bottom of dish by ½ inch and roast until soft (about 40 minutes depending on size of squash). Remove from oven and set aside. Reduce oven temperature to 250°F. When squash is cool enough to touch, hold over ovenproof serving dish and use tines of fork to scrape out flesh from top to bottom. Cover with foil and place in oven to keep hot.

In large skillet over medium heat, sauté onion and garlic in olive oil 3 minutes or until soft. Add capers, tomatoes and oregano and sauté 2 minutes. Fold in watercress and allow to wilt (about 30 seconds). Remove from heat, season to taste with salt and pepper and serve over spaghetti squash.

SERVES 6

Simple Stuffed Mochi with Bitter Greens

MOCHI IS MADE FROM PRESSED SWEET BROWN RICE and comes in a variety of flavors, including cinnamon raisin, plain and even chocolate (which is difficult to find but worth the effort!). Keep mochi in your refrigerator to use when you don't have time to prepare whole grains or as a nutritious alternative to bread. Mochi makes a great pocket for leftovers, chopped dried fruits and nuts and, of course, sautéed greens and vegetables, as I've done here.

12	fresh shiitake mushrooms
1	leek, sliced widthwise
1	tablespoon extra virgin olive oil
1	tablespoon Braggs Liquid Aminos or more as needed
1	cup grated carrots
1	cup grated daikon
1	tablespoon mirin
1	large bunch lacinato kale, chopped into bite-size pieces
1	tablespoon toasted sesame seeds
1	12.5-ounce package garlic or onion mochi, cut into 12 squares

Preheat oven to 350°F.

Prepare shiitake mushrooms by removing and discarding stems and slicing caps thinly. Set aside.

Heat large skillet to medium and sauté leek in olive oil until soft (about 3 minutes). Add shiitakes and continue sautéing. Add water or liquid aminos 1 tablespoon at a time to deglaze pan. Continue sautéing until mushrooms caramelize (8–10 minutes total). Add carrots, daikon and mirin and sauté until carrots are soft (4–5 minutes). Fold in kale and sauté 4 minutes or until tender. Remove from heat, toss with sesame seeds and set aside.

Place mochi squares on a parchment-lined baking sheet and bake until they puff (follow directions on package). Remove from oven, slice open each puff, stuff with sautéed greens and serve.

MAKES 12 stuffed mochi squares

Sun-Dried Tomato Infused Millet with Cured Olives and Herbs

MILLET IS A FAIRLY MILD GRAIN, but this preparation is anything but! My favorite way to serve this dish is with roasted portobello mushrooms — either stuffed into the cap, or with the mushroom sliced and served over the grain. The saltiness of the olives and the tanginess of the sun-dried tomatoes also make this a great accompaniment to sautéed greens and lemon or Provençal-style chicken, fish or tofu.

1	cup millet
6	sun-dried tomatoes, finely chopped
2	cups water
1	red onion, finely chopped
1	tablespoon extra virgin olive oil
1	tablespoon minced fresh rosemary (or 1 teaspoon dried)
1	tablespoon minced fresh thyme (or 1 teaspoon dried)
1	tablespoon minced fresh oregano (or 1 teaspoon dried)
2	teaspoons mirin
¼	cup chopped cured olives of choice
Freshly ground black pepper	

Place millet in fine-mesh strainer, rinse and drain.

Transfer millet to Dutch oven and dry roast over medium heat until fragrant (about 3 minutes). Add sun-dried tomatoes and water and bring to boil. Reduce heat to medium-low, cover and simmer until liquid is absorbed (about 25 minutes). Remove from heat (do not fluff) and set aside.

In medium skillet over medium heat, sauté onion in olive oil 3 minutes or until soft. Add herbs, mirin and olives and continue sautéing 2 minutes. Remove from heat.

Fluff millet with fork, fold in herb mixture, season to taste with pepper and serve.

TIPS

If you don't have all herbs on hand, substitute 1 tablespoon herbes de Provence, and garnish with chopped fresh flat-leaf parsley.

Pinto Beans with Stewed Tomatoes and Spinach

THIS IS YOUR NEW GO-TO RECIPE for those late-in-the-season tomatoes that are perfectly sweet but that look a bit worse for the wear. The first time I made this recipe I used canned tomatoes, but then my friend Ron in New Mexico told me about his grandmother, who used to make her pinto beans with a whole tomato. I am definitely not one to argue with tradition – let alone Grandma. So I immediately changed my recipe. As expected – she was right!

1	cup dried pinto beans
2½	cups vegetable stock
	Thumb-size piece kombu
¼	teaspoon ground cumin
2	medium tomatoes
1	yellow onion, chopped
2	cups packed spinach leaves
	Sea salt and freshly ground black pepper

Soak beans as desired according to instructions on page 13. Drain soaking water, rinse beans and drain well.

In Dutch oven over high heat, bring vegetable stock to boil. Add beans and kombu. When liquid returns to boil, skim off and discard any foam from top and reduce heat to medium-low. Add cumin and tomatoes (whole or chopped), cover and simmer 45 minutes.

Fold in chopped onion and spinach and season with salt and pepper. Cover and cook an additional 20 minutes or until nearly all liquid is absorbed. Remove from heat and serve.

SERVES 4

TIPS
You can use any variety of tomatoes that you like, but a nice juicy beefsteak style infuses this dish much more than the traditional plum tomatoes used for cooking. To take this dish into winter, substitute 1½ cups canned chopped tomatoes for the 2 whole tomatoes.

Sesame Forbidden Rice

THIS BLACK RICE IS SIMPLE, STRIKING AND RICH, and will surely make the rest of your meal visually pop. Imagine the variety of tastes, textures and colors when you serve it with pink-orange salmon, bright leafy greens and vibrant yellow sweet corn. It smells wonderful, looks wonderful and is a feast for all of your senses! For a completely different meal, serve this rice with Pan-Seared Tofu with Ginger Lime Glaze *(page 106)* and steamed bok choy.

---

1   cup forbidden black rice

2   cups water

Thumb-size piece kombu

2   tablespoons toasted
    sesame oil

¼   cup toasted sesame seeds

1   teaspoon
    ume plum vinegar

Rinse rice and place in pot with water and kombu. Bring to boil, reduce heat, cover and simmer until liquid is absorbed. Remove from heat and set aside to cool slightly. Remove and discard kombu, fluff rice and dress with sesame oil, sesame seeds and ume plum vinegar. Serve warm.

SERVES 4

TIP
Enjoy this rich grain dish as a salad by allowing your rice to cool first, then fluffing with a fork.

VARIATIONS
In the spring, fold in finely chopped garlic scapes, sugar snap peas and mandarin oranges. In summer, try chopped scallion and chopped peaches.

Veggie Hash

GROWING UP, my mother used to make "Goodness Soup" out of onions, carrots, grains, legumes – whatever she had on hand. Everything came together and simmered for hours until it was thick, creamy and delicious. This recipe employs the same "everything but the kitchen sink" approach – but without the liquid to turn it into soup!

1   medium yellow onion, diced

3   garlic cloves, minced

3   tablespoons grapeseed oil

2   cups grated sweet potatoes

2   cups grated potatoes (fingerling or other variety, peeled if necessary)

1   cup grated zucchini

1   cup grated yellow summer squash

¼   cup chopped fresh flat-leaf parsley

Sea salt and freshly ground black pepper

In large oven-proof skillet over medium heat, sauté onion and garlic in 1 tablespoon oil for 6 minutes or until caramelized. Add sweet potatoes and white potatoes and sauté 4 minutes. Place zucchini and summer squash in sieve over bowl. Press firmly to get rid of as much liquid as possible. Add to potatoes along with parsley, and season to taste with plenty of salt and pepper. Continue sautéing until vegetables are cooked through (10–12 minutes).

Turn broiler to high. Spread hash evenly across skillet, place under broiler and cook 6 minutes or until hash is crisp on the top (but not burnt) and soft on the inside. Remove from oven, flip hash, spread evenly in skillet and return to broiler for an additional 6 minutes or until crisp. Remove from oven and serve.

SERVES 4

VARIATIONS
If you prefer hash that holds together more, add 2 well-beaten eggs (or the equivalent egg replacer of choice) during the sauté. Spice this dish up with a few dashes of hot sauce.

SERVING SUGGESTIONS
Serve with refried pinto beans, or scrambled tofu or eggs. Enjoy it just as is, or top with red or green salsa, sliced avocado and/or guacamole.

Carrot Zucchini Muffins

I PREFER PIE TO CAKE AND MUFFINS ANY DAY of the year…except when I make this recipe. As is so often the case, this combination grew out of a craving, not only for a light, moist muffin with just the right combination of savory and sweet, but for a healthy snack that would make my children feel that Mommy baked something special just for them. It worked for me. I hope it works for you!

DRY INGREDIENTS

¾ cup chickpea flour

½ cup corn flour

½ cup almond meal

¼ cup potato starch

1 tablespoon baking powder

1 teaspoon baking soda

¼ teaspoon sea salt

¼ teaspoon ground nutmeg

¼ teaspoon ground cinnamon

WET INGREDIENTS

⅔ cup mashed banana (from about 1 large ripe banana)

¾ cup maple syrup

1 tablespoon lemon juice

½ teaspoon vanilla extract

¾ cup grated carrots

¾ cup grated zucchini

½ cup chopped toasted walnuts

½ cup dried currants or raisins

Preheat oven to 350°F and prepare mini-muffin tins with oil or paper muffin cups.

In large mixing bowl, whisk together all dry ingredients. In separate large bowl, whisk together banana, maple syrup, lemon juice and vanilla. Place grated carrots and zucchini together in a piece of cheesecloth or paper towel and squeeze out excess liquid. Add to wet ingredients along with walnuts and currants or raisins and stir to combine. Pour wet ingredients into dry and mix briefly to combine. Immediately scoop batter by tablespoonfuls into muffin tins. Distribute batter evenly. Bake 20 minutes or until toothpick inserted in center of muffin comes out clean. Remove from oven and set on wire rack to cool completely before removing from tins.

MAKES approximately 34 mini muffins

TIP
Muffins freeze well in an airtight container.

Pumpkin Spice Muffins

THESE MUFFINS, FULL OF MY FAVORITE warming spices, were a hit from the very beginning. The high-protein combination of flours used makes them a nutritious breakfast snack, and an extremely popular lunch box treat.

WET INGREDIENTS

1   cup pitted dates

1   tablespoon lemon juice

1½   cups cooked
     pumpkin purée

½   cup maple syrup

½   teaspoon vanilla extract

¼   cup almond butter

⅔   cup grated peeled apple or
     applesauce

DRY INGREDIENTS

½   cup brown teff flour

½   cup chickpea flour

½   cup almond meal

¼   cup potato starch

¼   teaspoon sea salt

1   tablespoon
     baking powder

1   teaspoon baking soda

1   teaspoon
     ground cinnamon

¼   teaspoon ground cloves

¼   teaspoon ground nutmeg

⅛   teaspoon ground allspice

Preheat oven to 350°F and prepare mini-muffin tins with oil or paper muffin cups.

Place dates in food processor and mince. Add remaining wet ingredients and process to combine. Place all dry ingredients in separate bowl, and whisk to combine.

Pour wet ingredients into dry and mix briefly to combine. Immediately scoop batter by the tablespoonful into muffin tins. Distribute batter evenly. Bake 20 minutes or until toothpick inserted in center comes out clean. Remove from oven and set on rack to cool completely before removing from tins.

MAKES approximately 30 mini muffins

TIP
Muffins freeze well in an airtight container.

Peanut Butter Balls

IT IS WELL KNOWN IN MY FAMILY that I love Reese's Peanut Butter Cups. My willpower holds me in good stead for most of the year, but Halloween can be a problem. Eating just one peanut butter cup is difficult, and multiple indulgences start an addiction that can be troublesome. Rather than face my problem, I decided to feed it and so I created this healthier alternative, which I like just as much as, if not more than, the original.

1   cup natural peanut butter

½   cup maple syrup

½   cup crispy rice cereal, plus more if needed

2   cups gluten- and dairy-free chocolate chips or 12 ounces dark chocolate

Place peanut butter and maple syrup in food processor and pulse to combine. Fold in crispy rice cereal. If your peanut butter is particularly runny, add more cereal until mixture holds together in balls. Form penny-size balls and place on parchment-lined cookie sheet.

Melt chocolate chips or chocolate in double boiler or in small pot over very low heat. Drop 3 or 4 balls at a time into chocolate and roll them around until covered completely. With a teaspoon, scoop out each ball individually, holding it against the side of the bowl to allow excess chocolate to drip off. Place each chocolate-covered ball back on lined cookie sheet. Repeat until all balls are coated and refrigerate until firm (at least 1 hour). Serve cold or room temperature.

MAKES 30 balls

VARIATION
For added nutritional value and a bit of welcome crunch, add ¼ cup cacao nibs to peanut butter and maple syrup when you add the crispy rice.

Baked Apples with Raisins and Toasted Almonds

THERE'S SOMETHING ABOUT BAKED APPLES that takes me back to my grandmother's kitchen. This recipe nourishes that memory and has the added benefit of filling my home and my heart with its wonderful aroma. It's much easier to serve than whole baked apples and is especially good with a dollop of vanilla rice cream or Greek yogurt.

4	baking apples of choice
½	cup sliced almonds
¼	cup raisins
½	cup maple syrup
½	cup apple cider or juice
2	teaspoons grated fresh ginger
2	teaspoons lemon juice
1	tablespoon lemon zest

Freshly grated nutmeg

Preheat oven to 350°F.

Halve apples and scoop out cores. Halve again and fit apples close together (flesh side up) in an 8 x 8-inch baking dish in one layer. Sprinkle almonds and raisins evenly over apples.

In small saucepan over medium heat, combine maple syrup, apple cider, ginger and lemon juice, and heat briefly. Remove from heat and pour evenly over apples. Sprinkle lemon zest and nutmeg evenly over the top, cover tightly with foil and bake 45 minutes or until apples are soft. Remove from oven and remove foil. Preheat broiler. Broil apples 1 minute to brown tops. Remove from oven, cool slightly and serve apples with extra cooking liquid as desired.

SERVES 6

VARIATIONS
Substitute pecans and dried cranberries for almonds and raisins. You can even substitute pears for apples.

WINTER

Heart Warming Winter Drinks

MY WEEKLY TRIPS TO THE FARM are always the source of great inspiration. Both of these recipes were created as a result of these visits. The coconut milk is a brew that one customer shared with me when I questioned the extraordinary amount of turmeric he was purchasing. He makes it as a medicinal brew, but I spiced it up to create this festive holiday treat. The tea, on the other hand, is my idea of a medicinal brew that's perfect on a cold day, and equally delicious served chilled in the heat of summer.

HOT SPICED COCONUT MILK

3 cups rice, almond or hemp milk

1½ cups coconut milk

1 tablespoon grated fresh turmeric

1 tablespoon grated fresh ginger

3 pieces star anise

3 cinnamon sticks

5 whole cloves

Zest of 1 orange

Freshly grated whole nutmeg

Place all ingredients except nutmeg in pot over high heat and whisk until smooth. Bring to gentle boil, reduce heat to low, cover and simmer 30 minutes. Remove from heat and serve hot, topped with nutmeg.

SERVES 6

GREEN TEA WITH LEMONGRASS AND GINGER

2 stalks lemongrass (bottom 4 inches only)

1-inch piece fresh ginger, peeled and chopped

4 cups water

4 green tea teabags

1 tablespoon pomegranate juice

Trim dry ends from lemongrass and discard. Peel outer leaves, and slice remaining stalks lengthwise into thin strips. Place in pot, add ginger and water and bring to boil. Reduce heat and simmer 10 minutes. Remove from heat, add teabags and steep 3–4 minutes (longer steeping will yield a more bitter tea). Remove tea bags, lemongrass and ginger and discard. Stir in pomegranate juice and serve.

SERVES 4

VARIATION

Chill and serve with a sprig of mint or lemon balm for a cool summer iced tea.

Shallot Fig Spread

YOU'RE GOING TO LOVE THIS VERSATILE SPREAD! Enjoy it as an appetizer or a snack on a rice cracker, thin it with water or orange juice for a savory marinade, or spread it on a rice tortilla, top with sautéed chard and broil for a yummy gourmet pizza.

---

1   cup dried Turkish figs (about 12)

2   cups water

7   shallots, peeled and thinly sliced

1   tablespoon extra virgin olive oil

1   tablespoon grated fresh ginger

Zest of 1 large orange

Juice of 2 oranges

2   tablespoons maple syrup

Prepare figs by discarding tough stem ends and cutting fruit into halves. Place in small pot over medium-high heat with 2 cups water and bring to boil. Simmer until liquid is reduced to ½ cup (about 20 minutes). Remove from heat and set aside, keeping figs in liquid.

Over medium heat, sauté shallots in olive oil until very soft (about 15 minutes). Add ginger, orange zest and juice. Stir continuously and sauté 5 minutes longer. Add figs, reduced liquid and maple syrup. Stir to combine and remove from heat. When cool enough to touch, transfer mixture into mixing bowl and gently purée with handheld blender (or food processor) until spread is blended but some figs and shallots are still visible. Cover and refrigerate at least 1 hour before serving.

MAKES 2 cups

Mango Chutney

IT CAN BE HARD TO SAY GOOD-BYE to the refreshing fruits and berries of summer. So I carry that sweetness into my winter menu with this chutney. I serve it as a spread on crackers, a topping to accompany fish or chicken, or thinned and used as a marinade for tofu. Add some bitter greens and you have a complete meal.

---

1 medium sweet onion, diced

2 stalks celery, diced

2 tablespoons grated fresh ginger

1 tablespoon grated fresh turmeric (or 1 teaspoon dried)

2 teaspoons virgin coconut oil

2 mangoes, peeled and diced

½ cup raisins

⅔ cup sweet white wine

2 tablespoons apple cider vinegar

1 teaspoon ground coriander

½ teaspoon ground cumin

¼ teaspoon ground cinnamon

Pinch of sea salt

In Dutch oven over medium heat, sauté onion, celery, ginger and turmeric in coconut oil until just soft (about 4 minutes). Add remaining ingredients and stir. When chutney starts to bubble, reduce heat to medium-low, cover and cook 30 minutes or until ingredients are soft and blended together. Remove cover and cook an additional 10 minutes to reduce liquids. Remove from heat, stir and set aside to cool. Stir before serving.

MAKES approximately 3 cups

TIPS

For best results, make this recipe in advance so that the flavors can blend and develop. For a more pungent finish, add a dash of ground cayenne before simmering. This recipe doubles easily and can be stored in the freezer in an airtight container.

Creamy Broccoli Soup

YOU CAN USE THIS RECIPE AS A TEMPLATE for any cream-style soup. For a whole new taste, try substituting spinach, parsnips or cannellini beans for the broccoli. Prepare whichever vegetable you select as your primary base and add it to the pot once the onion and garlic are soft.

---

2   garlic cloves, peeled

1   medium yellow onion, chopped

2   tablespoons extra virgin olive oil

1   large bunch broccoli (about 7 cups chopped)

2   cups rice milk

1   cup rolled oats

3   cups vegetable stock

¼   cup mellow white or chickpea miso

¼   cup water

In soup pot or large Dutch oven over medium heat, sauté garlic and onion in olive oil until soft (about 3 minutes).

Prepare broccoli by peeling stalks and discarding tough ends. Cut remaining stalks and tops into bite-size pieces and add to pot with onions and garlic. Add rice milk, oats, and vegetable stock. Bring to boil and stir, making sure all oats are submerged in stock. Reduce heat to medium, cover and simmer 10 minutes or until broccoli is soft. Remove from heat.

Using handheld blender or food processor, purée soup until smooth and creamy. In separate bowl, dissolve miso in water, stir into individual servings of slightly cooled soup and serve.

SERVES 6

TIP
Miso is a living food that helps replenish healthy intestinal flora but loses these health benefits when boiled. Always remove soup from heat and cool slightly before adding miso.

New Year's Soup

IN THE SOUTH IT'S BELIEVED that eating black-eyed peas and collard greens on New Year's Day ensures good luck and prosperity in the year ahead. This less traditional preparation is simple and soothing, without the ham hock often found in traditional "peas and greens." In my home we eat this soup all winter long, but on New Year's Day it especially provides welcome wholesomeness to balance the sweets of the holiday season.

1	medium yellow onion, chopped
4	garlic cloves, minced
1	tablespoon extra virgin olive oil
3	carrots, cut into ⅛-inch rounds (about 2 cups)
3	parsnips, cut into ⅛-inch rounds (about 1 cup)
1	bunch collard greens, stems removed
3	cups cooked black-eyed peas
2	tablespoons chopped fresh oregano
1½	cups chopped tomatoes
4	cups vegetable stock
1	tablespoon apple cider vinegar
	Sea salt and freshly ground black pepper

In soup pot or large Dutch oven over medium heat, sauté onion and garlic in olive oil 3 minutes or until soft. Add carrots and parsnips and sauté 3 minutes. Chop collard greens into bite-size pieces and add to pot along with black-eyed peas and oregano. Add chopped tomatoes and vegetable stock, bring to boil, reduce heat and simmer covered for 20–25 minutes. Stir in apple cider vinegar and season to taste with salt and pepper. Remove from heat and serve.

SERVES 6

SERVING SUGGESTION
For a heartier meal, stir 1 cup cooked quinoa or millet into soup before serving.

Sweet Potato and Cashew Soup with Avocado Cream

I FIRST TASTED THIS SOUP at a wonderful restaurant in Toronto, and I've been craving it ever since. I've altered it a bit by adding the avocado cream, but it's equally delicious with just a drizzle of sage or truffle oil as the garnish. The cashews provide a rich creaminess without actual cream, and you can make it completely free of tree nuts by using sunflower butter instead.

AVOCADO CREAM

1	garlic clove, peeled
2	avocados
¼	cup plain soy yogurt (or plain yogurt of choice)
3	tablespoons lime juice
¼	cup fresh cilantro leaves
¼	teaspoon sea salt

SOUP

1	medium onion, chopped
2	stalks celery, chopped
2	tablespoons grapeseed oil
3	medium sweet potatoes, peeled and chopped
1	cup cashews or cashew butter
5	cups vegetable stock
	Sea salt
½	cup chopped scallions

PREPARING AVOCADO CREAM

With food processor running, drop in garlic and process until minced. Halve avocados, and remove and save pits. Scoop out avocado flesh, add to processor and whip until smooth. Add yogurt, lime juice, cilantro and salt and process until evenly combined. Place in airtight container with pits to prevent browning and set aside or refrigerate until ready to serve.

PREPARING SOUP

In soup pot or large Dutch oven over medium heat, sauté onion and celery in oil until soft (4–6 minutes). Add sweet potatoes, cashews or cashew butter and vegetable stock. Bring to boil, reduce heat and simmer 20 minutes. Remove from heat and purée with handheld blender until smooth. Season to taste with salt and add stock or water to achieve desired consistency. Remove pit from cream and compose individual servings of soup with a dollop of avocado cream in each and a sprinkle of chopped scallions.

SERVES 4

Curried Cauliflower Stew with Chickpeas

I WAS ONCE THE GIRL WHO DIDN'T LIKE CAULIFLOWER, but this dish totally changed my tune. Cauliflower's mild flavor lends itself easily to a variety of spices and is the perfect complement to curry in particular. For an even heartier meal, I add steamed tempeh to this recipe and serve it with brown basmati rice and steamed mustard greens.

1   head cauliflower

1   medium yellow onion, sliced into thin wedges

2   garlic cloves, minced

1-inch piece fresh ginger, peeled and cut into matchsticks

1   tablespoon grapeseed oil

2   carrots, sliced into ¼-inch rounds

2   tablespoons mirin

1   tablespoon curry powder

1   cup vegetable stock

1½ cups chopped tomatoes with their juices

1½ cups cooked chickpeas

2   tablespoons raisins

Sea salt and freshly ground black pepper

Chopped fresh cilantro

Prepare cauliflower by removing and discarding outer leaves and inner stems. Cut florets into small pieces and set aside.

In Dutch oven over medium-high heat, sauté onion, garlic and ginger in oil until soft (about 3 minutes). Add carrots and sauté 2 minutes. Add mirin, curry powder, vegetable stock, tomatoes and chickpeas and stir to combine. Bring stew to simmer, fold in cauliflower and raisins and cook until cauliflower is soft (about 5 minutes). Season to taste with salt and pepper and serve topped with cilantro.

SERVES 4

Sweet Root Casserole with Dried Fruit

GROWING UP, I REMEMBER TZIMMES being my favorite dish at all of our holiday celebrations. As a child, I loved it because it was sweet and delicious, but as an adult it was simply too sweet. This new version features many more seasonal vegetables than my grandmother's traditional tzimmes and combines it all with pungent ginger and tart cherries for a dish that's hard to resist.

---

3 medium sweet potatoes, peeled

6 parsnips, peeled

5 carrots, peeled

1 small yellow onion, sliced into wedges

10 pitted prunes, halved

½ cup unsweetened dried cherries

2-inch piece fresh ginger, peeled and julienned

1 cup orange juice

¼ cup maple syrup

¼ cup lime juice

1 teaspoon arrowroot powder

⅛ teaspoon freshly grated nutmeg

Zest of 1 lemon, coarsely chopped

Sea salt

Preheat oven to 375°F.

Chop sweet potatoes, parsnips and carrots into 1-inch chunks and place in 9 x 13-inch casserole. Add onion, prunes, cherries and ginger and toss to evenly distribute ingredients. In separate bowl, combine orange juice, maple syrup, lime juice, arrowroot, nutmeg, lemon zest and salt. Whisk to combine ingredients and pour evenly over vegetables. Cover with foil and bake 45 minutes. Remove from oven, remove foil and baste. Return uncovered casserole to oven and bake another 15 minutes. Toss vegetables to recoat with thickening liquid and bake a final 15 minutes. Remove from oven, toss vegetables again to recoat with sauce and serve.

SERVES 8

VARIATIONS
One large butternut squash can be substituted for the sweet potatoes, parsnips and carrots. If you have leftovers, heat them in a pot with just enough vegetable stock to cover and lightly purée for a sweet root vegetable soup with a refreshing, tart finish.

Herb Roasted Cauliflower with Shiitake Mushrooms

WHEN I FIRST DISCOVERED how creamy and smooth cauliflower became when puréed, I knew it had much more potential than I had given it credit for in my cauliflower-hating youth. Now, I can hardly get enough. The caramelized mushrooms and Brussels sprouts in this recipe are a winning combination, and roasting brings out the earthy taste of the cauliflower even more. Serve it with French lentils or wild rice for a warm and tasty winter meal.

---

1 large head cauliflower

1½ dozen Brussels sprouts

½ pound shiitake mushrooms

2 garlic cloves, peeled

¼ cup fresh sage leaves
(or 1½ tablespoons dried)

¼ cup fresh oregano
(or 1½ tablespoons dried)

2 teaspoons coarse sea salt

¼ cup extra virgin olive oil

Preheat oven to 400°F.

Prepare cauliflower by removing and discarding outer leaves and inner stems. Cut florets into small pieces and place in large mixing bowl. Prepare Brussels sprouts by cutting away and discarding dry ends. Halve sprouts and place in bowl with cauliflower. Remove stems from shiitake mushroom caps, slice caps into ¼ inch strips and add to vegetables.

With food processor running, drop in garlic cloves and process until minced. Add sage, oregano, salt and oil and pulse briefly to chop herbs and blend ingredients. Remove from processor bowl and fold into vegetables to coat evenly. Transfer to baking dish and roast 15 minutes. Remove from oven, toss to redistribute and prevent burning, and roast an additional 15–20 minutes or until tender. Remove from oven and serve.

SERVES 4

TIP
If Brussels sprouts are particularly large, you may want to cut them into quarters instead of halves.

Jerusalem Artichokes with Lemon and Rosemary

ALSO REFERRED TO AS A "SUNCHOKE," this high-iron root vegetable is a nice alternative to potatoes and brings with it a welcome crunch. Serve them on their own or toss finished chokes with steamed collard greens or kale for a heartier and more colorful side dish.

8–10 Jerusalem artichokes

2 tablespoons extra virgin olive oil

4 garlic cloves, minced

2 tablespoons lemon juice

1 tablespoon minced fresh rosemary (or 1 teaspoon dried)

Sea salt and freshly ground black pepper

Scrub artichokes well and slice widthwise. Place cast-iron skillet over medium heat. Add olive oil and sliced chokes and sauté 2–3 minutes. Add garlic and lemon juice and continue sautéing 4–5 minutes. Deglaze pan with 1 tablespoon water at a time, as needed. Add rosemary, salt and pepper and sauté 1 minute longer or until chokes are caramelized. Remove from heat, add more salt and pepper as desired and serve.

SERVES 4

Sesame Miso Tofu with Asian Greens

THIS MAY LOOK LIKE A SINGLE RECIPE, but in fact it delivers tons of options that my family loves. I regularly make the marinated tofu to accompany rice and greens, to stuff into sandwiches, or simply to snack on. And I like to serve the stir-fried vegetables over forbidden rice or noodles, alongside a piece of grilled salmon and, of course, tossed with the sesame miso tofu as I've done here. Hardly a week goes by when I haven't used this recipe — one way or another.

1   pound firm tofu
     (not silken)

MARINADE
2   tablespoons mellow
     white miso
2   tablespoons tahini
2   tablespoons
     grated fresh ginger
2   tablespoons
     brown rice vinegar
2   tablespoons maple syrup
     or brown rice syrup
¼   cup water

STIR FRY
½   medium yellow onion,
     cut into wedges
2   tablespoons grapeseed oil
1   cup julienned carrots
1   cup snow peas
2   cups chopped bok choy
4   cups chopped
     Napa cabbage
1   tablespoon tamari
1   tablespoon mirin
1½   cups mung bean sprouts,
     rinsed well
Toasted sesame oil

Wrap tofu in towel and gently press out excess liquid. Cut tofu into 1-inch cubes and place in 8-inch square casserole. In mixing bowl, whisk together all marinade ingredients. Pour over tofu and marinate 30 minutes.

Preheat oven to 400°F. Transfer tofu to clean baking dish and roast 15 minutes. Do not discard marinade. Remove from oven, flip tofu pieces, coat with more marinade and return to oven to roast an additional 15 minutes. Remove from oven and set aside until ready to stir-fry.

In wok or Dutch oven over high heat, stir-fry onion in 1 tablespoon oil 2 minutes. Add carrots and snow peas and stir-fry 1 minute or until bright orange and green. Remove all vegetables from wok and set aside. Add remaining tablespoon oil to wok and stir-fry bok choy and Napa cabbage 1 minute or until wilted. Fold in carrots, snow peas and tofu. Add tamari and mirin, toss and remove from heat. Add bean sprouts, drizzle with toasted sesame oil, toss and serve.

SERVES 4

TIP
To yield firmer tofu, allow it to sit briefly after roasting.

VARIATION
Substitute steamed tempeh for the tofu. Experiment with toppings such as chopped scallion, dry roasted peanuts, gomasio or hot sesame oil.

Kabocha Squash and Sprouts with Pears and Pomegranate

KOBACHA SQUASH CAN BE QUITE DECEPTIVE with its tough-looking skin, but in actuality it's tender, hearty and deliciously sweet – skin and all! Because kabocha does not require peeling, it is particularly easy to prepare. The dark green skin and bright orange flesh provide beautiful color contrast, and its slightly dry, sweet taste is a great complement to the other flavors and textures in this dish.

---

1   kabocha squash, halved and seeded

12   Brussels sprouts, trimmed

3   ripe pears

1   large leek, chopped widthwise

2   tablespoons pomegranate juice

2   tablespoons extra virgin olive oil

1   tablespoon maple syrup

⅛   teaspoon freshly grated nutmeg

1   teaspoon coarse sea salt

½   cup toasted walnuts

Seeds from ½ pomegranate

Preheat oven to 400°F.

Cut squash, Brussels sprouts and pears into equal bite-size pieces and place in 9 x 13-inch casserole. Add leek and toss to combine. In small bowl, whisk together pomegranate juice, olive oil, maple syrup and nutmeg. Pour over vegetables and toss to coat. Roast 20 minutes. Remove from oven, toss to ensure even roasting and return to oven for 20 minutes longer or until squash is soft. Roasting time will depend on the size of the cut vegetables. Remove from oven, sprinkle with salt and walnuts and serve topped with pomegranate seeds.

SERVES 6

VARIATIONS

Delicata squash is another winter squash that does not require peeling and can be substituted easily for the kabocha, as can peeled butternut squash.

Wild Rice with Lemon, Fennel and Dried Plums

WILD RICE IS A GREAT SOURCE OF PROTEIN. As a runner, I especially appreciate the great long-lasting energy it provides without making me feel weary or sluggish. In fact, I tend to include wild rice in my dinner the night before a long run, bike ride or hike, as it's great fuel and tastes delicious!

1　cup wild rice

2½　cups vegetable stock

Pinch of sea salt

½　fennel bulb, finely chopped

4　cloves garlic, minced

2　tablespoons extra virgin olive oil

¾　cup chopped dried plums (prunes)

2　tablespoons mirin

1　tablespoon fresh thyme leaves

1　tablespoon chopped fresh sage

Juice and zest of 1 lemon

¼　cup chopped fresh flat-leaf parsley

½　cup toasted pine nuts

Rinse rice and place in pot with vegetable stock and salt. Turn heat to high and bring to boil. Reduce heat to medium-low, cover and simmer until liquid is absorbed (about 45 minutes). Remove from heat and set aside, but do not fluff yet.

In large Dutch oven over medium heat, sauté fennel and garlic in oil until soft (about 6 minutes). Stir in dried plums and mirin and continue sautéing 3 minutes. Deglaze pan as needed with water 1 tablespoon at a time. Add thyme and sage and stir. Fluff wild rice with wooden spoon and add to pot. Add lemon juice and zest and fold to incorporate. Continue sautéing until rice is heated through. Remove from heat, toss with parsley and pine nuts and serve.

SERVES 4

VARIATIONS

Substitute basmati, jasmine or forbidden black rice for the wild rice.

SERVING SUGGESTIONS

I usually serve this recipe as a side dish, but it can also be used as a stuffing for cabbage rolls or roasted squash.

Deep Dish Greens with Millet Amaranth Crust

WHEN MY CHILDREN WERE YOUNG, I made this one-dish meal with frozen veggies and a more traditional pie crust. As they became more adventurous eaters, I added more dark leafy greens, and eventually exchanged the crust for this hearty whole-grain topping. I'm not sure my family even remembers the original version, but they definitely love what it has become.

TOPPING
¾   cup combined millet and amaranth

2   cups vegetable stock

¼   teaspoon sea salt

2   tablespoons chopped dried parsley

Freshly ground black pepper

Extra virgin olive oil

FILLING
1   medium yellow onion, chopped

1   tablespoon grapeseed oil

3   carrots, chopped

1½   cups frozen peas

1½   cups frozen corn

2   tablespoons mirin

1   bunch kale, chopped

1   bunch collard greens, chopped

1   cup water

2   tablespoons tamari

1   tablespoon arrowroot powder

Place millet and amaranth in pot or rice cooker with vegetable stock and salt. Bring to boil, cover, reduce heat and simmer until all liquid is absorbed. Remove from heat and set aside.

In large Dutch oven over medium heat, sauté onion in oil 3 minutes or until soft. Add carrots, peas and corn and continue sautéing to heat through. Add mirin, fold in kale and collards, and sauté until tender and bright green. In small mixing bowl, whisk together water, tamari and arrowroot. Pour over vegetables, stir until sauce starts to thicken and remove from heat. Transfer to pie plate or casserole and set aside.

Turn on broiler.

When grains are done, fold in dried parsley and season to taste with salt and plenty of black pepper. Stir to combine and spread evenly over vegetables. Drizzle with olive oil and broil 5 minutes to yield a creamy grain topping with a crisp crust. Remove from oven and serve hot.

SERVES 4

VARIATION
Substitute polenta for grains and 1½ cups chopped tomatoes with their juices for 1 cup water and tamari.

Vegetable Medley with Chiles

ROASTING IS AN EASY WAY TO PREPARE a variety of winter vegetables, from roots and tubers to squashes and cabbages. The addition of habanero peppers gives this dish extra heat, which is always welcome on a cold day. If habaneros are too hot for your taste, substitute serranos, jalapeños or even crushed red pepper flakes.

3   medium sweet potatoes or yams

1   pound Brussels sprouts, ends trimmed

5   parsnips, peeled

4   shallots, quartered

8   garlic cloves, peeled

4   small hot chiles of choice

Extra virgin olive oil

Coarse sea salt

Preheat oven to 400°F.

Prepare sweet potatoes, Brussels sprouts and parsnips by chopping into ½-inch pieces. Place sweet potatoes, Brussels sprouts, parsnips, shallots and garlic in extra-large mixing bowl. Halve chiles lengthwise and discard seeds. Add to bowl and drizzle with enough olive oil to coat all vegetables lightly. Toss to combine, and spread vegetables into two 9 x 13-inch glass casseroles. Roast 15 minutes. Remove from heat, toss to ensure even cooking and prevent burning and return to oven for another 15 minutes or until vegetables are soft. Remove from heat, season to taste with salt and serve.

SERVES 4

Sautéed Kale with Red Onions and Cannellini Beans

I TRY TO PREPARE A BIG VAT OF GREENS at the beginning of each week. I serve them simply the first night. The second night, I sauté leeks or onions and add some beans, as I've done here – the rich and creamy cannellinis are my favorite. If there are any leftovers after that, I like to reheat them with chopped tomatoes and toss with pasta. Three great meals, all from just minutes of preparation.

1   red onion, peeled and cut into wedges

4   garlic cloves, minced

1   tablespoon chopped fresh rosemary

2   tablespoons extra virgin olive oil, plus more for drizzling

2   bunches kale, chopped

2   tablespoons mirin

3   cups cooked cannellini beans, rinsed

Ume plum vinegar

In Dutch oven over medium heat, sauté onion, garlic and rosemary in olive oil until soft (about 3 minutes). Add kale and mirin and sauté 4–5 minutes or until kale is bright green and tender. Add beans and sauté 2 minutes longer to heat through. Remove from heat, drizzle with olive oil, season to taste with ume plum vinegar, toss and serve.

SERVES 4

VARIATIONS
Chopped collard greens are a simple substitute for the kale in this recipe. To stray a little further, substitute chickpeas for the cannellinis and season with tamari.

French Lentils with Roasted Roots, Caramelized Onions and Thyme

LENTILS ARE A PERFECT COMPLEMENT to winter's colorful and sweet roots and squashes. Not only are they a great source of protein, but their somewhat earthy and savory taste enhances a variety of winter meals. Although there are three main steps required to make this recipe, the prep time is minimal. This dish goes great with sautéed mustard greens, kale and/or collards.

1	rutabaga, peeled and diced
1	celeriac (celery root), peeled and diced
4	tablespoons extra virgin olive oil
¾	cup dry French lentils
3	cups vegetable stock or water
Sea salt	
4	tablespoons lemon juice
1	large red onion, diced
4	cups thinly sliced mushrooms (variety of choice), about 1 pound
1	tablespoon mirin
2	tablespoons fresh thyme leaves, minced
Chopped fresh parsley	

Preheat oven to 400°F.

Place rutabaga and celeriac in 8 x 8-inch baking dish, drizzle with 2 tablespoons olive oil and roast 20 minutes. Remove from oven and toss. Return to oven and roast an additional 20 minutes or until soft. Remove from oven and set aside.

While vegetables are roasting, rinse lentils and place in pot with vegetable stock and a pinch of salt. Bring to boil, reduce heat, cover and simmer until just tender (about 20 minutes). Remove from heat and drain well. Toss with 1 tablespoon oil and 1 tablespoon lemon juice and set aside.

In large skillet over medium heat, sauté onion in remaining tablespoon olive oil until it starts to brown (5–7 minutes). Add mushrooms and mirin and continue sautéing. Add remaining 3 tablespoons lemon juice 1 tablespoon at a time to deglaze pan and caramelize vegetables. Add thyme and sauté 2 minutes longer, for a total sauté time of 12–14 minutes. Fold in lentils and roasted vegetables and sauté to heat through. Season to taste with salt, toss with parsley and serve.

SERVES 6

Millet in the Pot with Aduki Beans and Collards

THIS IS A ONE-POT, SUPER-WARMING and strengthening meal that's easy to prepare, rich in color and satisfying. Experiment with different grains, greens and legumes to find your favorite combination. To make this dish even simpler – start your grains in a rice cooker and after 10 minutes, add beans and vegetables. When the rice cooker turns off, stir everything together, season and serve.

1	cup millet
2	cups vegetable stock
½	yellow onion, cut into ¼-inch wedges
2	carrots, sliced into ⅛-inch rounds
1	cup cooked aduki beans, rinsed
1	bunch collard greens, chopped into bite-size pieces
1–2	tablespoons extra virgin olive oil
5–6	dashes ume plum vinegar
¼	cup toasted pumpkin seeds

Place millet in fine-mesh strainer, rinse and drain. Heat Dutch oven to medium, add millet to dry pot and stir 3–4 minutes to toast. Add vegetable stock and bring to boil. Cover, reduce heat and simmer 12 minutes. Keep millet on burner, open pot and evenly layer onion, carrots, beans and collard greens on top of millet (do not stir). Cover, increase heat to medium and continue cooking 20 minutes longer or until liquid is absorbed. Remove from heat, drizzle with olive oil and ume plum vinegar and fold to combine all ingredients. Serve topped with pumpkin seeds.

SERVES 4

VARIATION
Another favorite combination for this recipe is brown basmati rice, kidney beans and a combination of kale and mustard greens.

Glazed Tempeh and Sweet Vegetables

THIS SAVORY DISH IS LOADED WITH FLAVOR and comes together in no time. Enjoy it on its own for a light but satisfying meal or serve it over rice and bitter greens such as bok choy, dandelion or mustard greens for a more filling combination.

---

8 ounces tempeh, cut into bite-size cubes

15 Brussels sprouts, quartered

3 carrots, finely chopped

3 parsnips, finely chopped

2 tablespoons grapeseed oil

1 tablespoon grated fresh ginger

1 tablespoon grated fresh turmeric (or 1 teaspoon dried)

2 tablespoons mirin

1 cup freshly squeezed orange juice

2 tablespoons maple syrup

2 tablespoons red wine vinegar

2 teaspoons ground cumin

Sea salt and freshly ground black pepper

Chopped fresh flat-leaf parsley

Steam tempeh 5 minutes and set aside.

In Dutch oven over medium heat, sauté Brussels sprouts, carrots and parsnips in oil 2 minutes. Add ginger, turmeric and mirin and sauté 2 minutes longer.

In small mixing bowl, combine orange juice, maple syrup, red wine vinegar and cumin. Add tempeh and orange juice mixture to vegetables and stir to combine. Cover and reduce heat to medium. Simmer 10–12 minutes or until liquid is reduced to glaze and vegetables are soft. Season to taste with salt and pepper. Remove from heat, fold in parsley and serve.

SERVES 4

Cinnamon Whole Oats with Toasted Almonds

LABELING FOODS AS APPROPRIATE for breakfast, lunch or dinner feels too limiting to me. Sometimes I find last night's leftovers to be the best fuel for starting my day. And by day's end, often what I really want is simple comfort food. Whether you're looking for breakfast, lunch or dinner, this dish of hearty whole oats is sweet and satisfying and will warm your soul.

---

1 cup whole oats
(also known as oat groats)

2½ cups water

Pinch of sea salt

Flax oil

Maple syrup

Ume plum vinegar

1 cup toasted sliced almonds

Place oats in bowl, add enough water to cover and soak for at least 1 hour. When ready to cook, drain soaking water, rinse and drain again.

Place oats in pot with water and salt. Bring to boil, reduce heat to medium-low, cover and cook until all liquid is absorbed (50–55 minutes). To prevent pot from bubbling over, keep lid open slightly.

Remove pot from heat, fluff with wooden spoon and season to taste with a drizzle of flax oil, maple syrup and a dash of ume plum vinegar. Top with toasted almonds and serve.

SERVES 4

VARIATIONS
This recipe works great for amaranth and teff as well. Simply substitute for the whole oat groats and reduce water by ½ cup. For a sweeter finished dish, add 3 tablespoons currants, raisins or dried goji berries to pot and cook with grain, or cook grain with half water and half apple juice or cider. Optional garnishes include grated apple, ground cinnamon, orange zest or almond milk.

Buttercup Squash with Quinoa, Apricot and Sage Stuffing

SWEET WINTER SQUASHES MAKE BEAUTIFUL and delicious vessels for stuffing, and there are so many varieties to choose from. Buttercup is one of my favorites, but I also like to make this recipe with carnival, delicata and acorn varieties. While this savory stuffing pairs well with sweet squash, it also makes a nice stuffing for rolled cabbage or collard greens.

---

2 small buttercup squashes

2 tablespoons extra virgin olive oil, plus more for rubbing squash

1 cup quinoa

1½ cups water or vegetable stock

Pinch of sea salt

6 shallots, chopped

2 stalks celery, chopped

6 dried apricots, chopped

2 tablespoons chopped fresh sage

2 tablespoons chopped fresh parsley, plus whole sprigs for serving

1 tablespoon mirin

Zest of 1 lemon

2 tablespoons lemon juice

Sea salt and freshly ground black pepper

½ cup toasted sliced almonds

Preheat oven to 375°F.

Wash squash and cut in half or quarters, depending on desired serving size. Scoop out and discard seeds, rub skins with olive oil and place open-side down on parchment-lined baking pan. Roast 25 minutes or until soft throughout. Turn off heat, but leave squash in oven to stay warm until ready to serve.

Meanwhile, place quinoa in pot or rice cooker with water or vegetable stock and salt. Bring to boil, reduce heat, and simmer covered until liquid is absorbed (about 15 minutes). Remove from heat and set aside, but do not fluff yet.

In Dutch oven over medium heat, sauté shallots and celery in 1 tablespoon olive oil until soft. Add apricots, sage, parsley and mirin and sauté 3 minutes longer. Fluff quinoa and fold into shallot mixture. Add lemon zest and juice and remaining tablespoon olive oil and sauté 3 minutes longer or until heated through. Remove quinoa from heat and season to taste with salt and pepper. Remove squash from oven. Fill individual squash boats with stuffing, garnish with toasted almonds and parsley sprigs and serve.

SERVES 4

Orange Chocolate Mousse

EVERYBODY LOVED MY TRADITIONAL CHOCOLATE MOUSSE, but when I introduced this variation, that one was quickly forgotten. The hint of orange was so unexpected and so welcome, it elevated this recipe to family-favorite status immediately. You can serve it in a parfait glass or tart shell, or sneak it directly from the food processor like my children do!

---

12 ounces extra-firm silken tofu

½ teaspoon orange extract

¼ cup maple syrup

¾ cup gluten- and dairy-free chocolate chips or 4½ ounces dark chocolate

1 cup toasted slivered almonds

2 tablespoons grated orange zest

Wrap tofu in towel and gently press out excess liquid. Place in food processor and whip until smooth, scraping down sides of bowl as needed. Add orange extract and maple syrup and pulse to combine.

Melt chocolate chips or chocolate in double boiler or in small pot over very low heat. Remove from heat, add to tofu mixture and process until blended and smooth. Transfer to serving bowl or individual parfait glasses and refrigerate to chill. Remove from refrigerator, top with toasted almonds and orange zest and serve.

SERVES 4

Pear Cake

THE INSPIRATION FOR THIS RECIPE came from my friend Vicki, who is hands-down the best baker I know. Her super-moist apple cake is just the right combination of light and sweet. And, while I've still not been able to convince her to share her recipe, this gluten-free pear version satisfied my craving with ease. I would like to think that someday Vicki might actually ask me for this recipe, but I guess that's unnecessary now!

DRY INGREDIENTS
1 cup chickpea flour
1 cup almond meal
½ cup potato starch
1 tablespoon baking powder
1 teaspoon baking soda
¼ teaspoon sea salt
¼ teaspoon ground cinnamon

WET INGREDIENTS
1 cup finely grated peeled D'Anjou pear (or pear sauce)
1½ cups coarsely grated peeled D'Anjou pears
½ cup mashed banana (about 1 large banana)
½ cup maple syrup
2 tablespoons lemon juice
1 teaspoon almond or vanilla extract

TOPPING
1–2 D'Anjou pears

Preheat oven to 350°F and lightly grease a 9-inch springform pan.

In large mixing bowl, whisk together all dry ingredients until blended. In separate bowl, whisk together all wet ingredients until blended.

Peel pears for topping and cut into halves. Scoop out cores and slice halves into thin slices and set aside.

Pour wet ingredients into dry and mix as briefly as possible to combine. Pour into prepared pan. Arrange pear slices as desired on top of cake and bake 45 minutes or until cake is lightly browned on top and a toothpick inserted in the center comes out clean. Remove from oven and cool on rack before removing pan.

MAKES one 9-inch round cake

TIP
This recipe will require 5 or 6 whole pears, depending on the size of your pears – 2 for finely grating, 2 for coarsely grating and 1–2 for decorating the top of your cake.

SERVING SUGGESTION
For an extra-special presentation, melt dark chocolate with a small amount of virgin coconut oil and drizzle back and forth across each serving.

Cocoa Brownies

WHEN I FIRST STARTED BAKING I used lots of sugar, butter, white flour… and an Easy Bake Oven. Once I took out all the ingredients that make baked goods so delectable (and addicting), things got a little more challenging. When I started approaching baking more like cooking and less like chemistry (not one of my better subjects), my results definitely improved. These brownies taste like they're full of sinful ingredients, and you don't have to tell a soul that they're not!

½   cup grated apple
     or applesauce

8   pitted dates

1   ripe banana

½   cup maple syrup

1   teaspoon vanilla extract

½   cup brown teff flour

½   cup almond meal

½   cup cocoa powder

2   teaspoons baking powder

½   teaspoon baking soda

¼   teaspoon salt

Preheat oven to 350°F and lightly grease 8 x 8-inch baking dish.

In food processor, combine applesauce, dates, banana, maple syrup and vanilla until almost smooth, but with some chunks of dates remaining. In separate bowl, combine teff flour, almond meal, cocoa powder, baking powder, baking soda and salt. Pour wet ingredients into dry and mix as briefly as possible to incorporate all ingredients. Transfer to prepared baking dish and bake 25 minutes or until top appears slightly dry. Remove from oven and place on wire rack to cool completely before cutting and removing from pan.

MAKES 16 ooey, gooey brownies

INDEX